STRESS REPROGRAMMED

**A ten part interactive manual to help
you move from stress to success!**

by

David R Cotterill

*Personal Development Coach, NLP Master
Practitioner and Hypnotherapist*

**Grosvenor House
Publishing Limited**

This book is published by
Grosvenor House Publishing Ltd
28-30 High Street, Guildford, Surrey, GU1 3EL.
www.grosvenorhousepublishing.co.uk

A CIP record for this book
is available from the British Library

ISBN 978-1-908596-59-8

Contents

Acknowledgements

I would like to thanks some very important people who have influenced, inspired and encouraged me in the writing of this book.

Without the voice of Paul McKenna via a CD that came with his book "Instant Confidence" I may never have started my journey to freedom from stress. I thank Paul for this and his subsequent training and a huge thank you to his mentor Dr Richard Bandler, co-creator of NLP and also Michael Neil for his part as a supercoach trainer and John and Kathleen LaValle for their work with NLP Life.

A huge thanks to Dr Jay Lehr for inspiring me to finish the work and his wife Janet for supporting him in being the amazing man he is. Thanks to my family GP Dr Phil Harriram for his encouragement and to Mark, Jill and the class of 2008 at Uncommon Knowledge for putting up with me during the early days of my journey of self-discovery through hypnosis and "trance-formation".

Thanks to all my clients, friends, colleagues who have been willing and not-so-willing participants in this work and to my precious "family" past, present and future – Fred, Barbara, Sonia, Stuart, Samantha, Ruth, Deborah, Doreen, Michelle and Ben, Charlotte, Emily, anyone I have not mentioned and those who have yet to know me.

Finally thanks to Sandra, Tom and all at CCTS who are presently helping me in the next phase of my journey.

God bless you all and wherever you are may you never tire of striving to be the best you can.

Disclaimer

Introduction

"Break Out" Exercises

Throughout this book there are exercises that will help you to change your perspectives, the way you interpret the incoming data from the world and re-present it in your mind.

They are referred to as "Break Out" exercises because they will require you to "break out" from reading the book for a while, but they will also begin to enable you to "break out" from old unhealthy patterns of behaviour and kick start your new life.

The exercises will also help you to take control over the way your mind works in terms of imagining future events or interpreting the past.

These exercises sometimes involve closing your eyes, relaxing and, at times, entering a mild trance state similar to that sometimes experienced in therapeutic hypnosis.

This is a natural state that we all enter into at times on a daily basis.

For example, when we concentrate on a physical activity, such as sport or exercising we can quite easily slip into trance. It also helps us to concentrate during methodical activities or boring periods.

Some might refer to it as daydreaming.

If we read a book, watch a movie or listen to music, we can trance out and that activity can become more "real" for a time than our everyday life.

Many people experience, when driving, having arrived at a destination or travelled for some time, without realising they had done it. This is trance.

What this also indicates is that there is a deeper consciousness, what I will refer to as the unconscious mind, which is "watching over us" and keeping an eye out for hidden dangers if we "drift off".

How often do you remember something that you were not concentrating on but were aware of in your peripheral vision and "registered" by your unconscious mind to be recalled later?

Conversely, you may not be able to remember something you thought you'd concentrated on remembering, only for it to suddenly "bubble up" later or during sleep?

Recent advances in brain scanning technology have enable us to understand and consequently utilise some of these phenomena and the many short exercises in the book will begin to utilise these natural resources to "re-programme" your brain to enable you to unlock those resources to manage your life better and beat stress.

Because many exercises involve relaxation it is recommended that you read them through in their entirety before deciding if you will work with a partner or record them to playback.

It will be beneficial to get someone else to read them gently and calmly aloud as you work through them and if you record them and listen back using speakers or, even better, headphones this will relax you too.

After a time your unconscious mind will pick up on the new "patterns" we're introducing through these exercises.

You will become acquainted with the therapeutic pattern of induction – that's a term meaning to go into relaxation – and your mind will bring you back out, refreshed and alert when you are ready.

However for the first few times if you are not working with a partner, it may be an idea to set an alarm for 5 minutes in case you fall asleep. This could happen the first few times, especially if you haven't relaxed deeply for some time.

Just relaxing can be incredibly beneficial to your overall well being.

Be careful, make sure you are in a comfortable place and position and that, in the event of you going to sleep, there are no dangers such as headphone cords or that you've not left something cooking!

A lot of health and safety is common sense, but be aware, prepare and the knowledge that you are safe will help you to relax.

The outcomes from these exercises will be most beneficial if you record them and listen back.

At first, you may find it strange to listen to your own voice.

However, you listen to your own voice much more than you realise, every day.

When you "negotiate" with yourself over things you have to do, or decisions you have to make it's your own voice that you hear but sometimes your inner voice will take on the vocal image of an authority figure such as a parent or teacher.

Many people have their behaviour influenced by such authority voices from their past which actually do not exist in reality, they are just simulations from their own mind – echoes of a real event which are sometimes blown out of proportion or arise out of the original context.

Some of the exercises in this book will offer you a choice over your future behaviour. You will find that you are less likely to be driven by voices from the past and able to choose new behavioural patterns that will be beneficial to you and your life goals.

Hypnosis works well because the hypnotist is able to communicate positive suggestions directly to the listener's unconscious mind. It may, at first, be a strange experience listening to such suggestions from your own recorded voice, but stick with it. If you find that you don't get the results you desire, ask a friend or partner to record the exercises for you.

After each exercise, you might find it useful to think of something completely different from that which you had been imagining. For example, you could imagine watching sausages sizzling away in a pan or maybe standing atop a windswept cliff overlooking the sea or perhaps playing tennis on a warm sunny day – anything that gets your conscious mind to suddenly change gear.

If you fully engage with any imagined experience, smell the aromas and immerse yourself in the sights and sounds, the change of orientation, which is a natural phenomenon that happens every day when you're attention is suddenly captured by a sudden movement or noise, will clear your mind almost like pressing a reset button or rebooting your computer.

It will also keep your mind alert and train you to become more able to respond to changes in your environment.

In your mind you have an incredibly powerful "Reality Simulator" and you will learn how to utilise this to create the life that's beneficial for you.

Finally, in order to measure changes, it is important to grade or scale your feelings before and after each exercise. Ask yourself, on a scale of 1-10, how you feel about the situation beforehand and again afterwards.

Assumptions on the nature of the human mind

The Conscious & Unconscious Mind

Throughout this book, and the exercises within it, are references to the conscious and unconscious mind.

From a therapeutic point of view it will be extremely valuable to work through this book using the assumption that the human mind consists of these two parts that operate in different but complimentary ways.

Many people use the term "subconscious" which is interchangeable with "unconscious" if that feels better for you.

There are some basic assumptions regarding the conscious and unconscious mind which I adhere to will help when working through the book and exercises:

The unconscious mind is distinct and separate from the conscious mind.

It co-exists with the conscious mind totally separate processes of awareness, response and learning.

The unconscious has its own stored memories, understandings and interests.

It can control physical activities without the conscious being aware of it (breathing / pulse etc.) and as a result can communicate with others outside of the range of conscious awareness.

The unconscious can act autonomously but generally will support and enhance the operations of the conscious mind.

So before we start, there is just a further word of advice.

Not all of the ideas and exercises will suit everybody.

Human beings are individuals and each of us has a unique understanding and perception of the universe in which we live and move and have our being.

If you find one aspect of perception that "fits" your world view and feels comfortable for you, then stick with it. If you find one that doesn't fit with your world-view then just let it go. Maybe you can revisit this later.

Use what's good for you.

Identifying Your Stress Triggers

What hits your stress button?

Have you ever stopped to think about where your stress is coming from?

Could it be your job?

Could it be your boss?

Maybe it's your partner?

Perhaps it's your kids?

Could be it's your parents?

Or maybe it's just your "situation"!

It certainly seems to be caused by some external factor, doesn't it?

Maybe it involves one person or another you come into contact with on a daily or regular basis?

As an active human being, part of a community within a society, it is impossible to avoid contact with other people.

How many people do you think you meet or interact with on an average day throughout your life?

If you work in an office, attend school or college you will perhaps interact with anything from 1 to 50. If you work in retail or sales you will probably meet many, many more.

Let's say that on your average day, maybe, you meet about 25 other people.

Add to that number, those you meet when socialising at weekends and evenings.

What about your years spent in education (both you and your kids if you have any)?

The number of "meetings" or encounters with other people could actually rise to hundreds of thousands!

During each and every one of those meetings, people could have influenced your mood at that time by their words and behaviour.

You may be considering that my case is flawed because clearly I have counted the same people we meet on a daily basis many times over, but consider this; almost every one of those people could well be in a different mood each time we meet with them. They could be happy in the morning, but moody by the afternoon and then completely miserable by the end of the day!

If you meet someone at the weekend, perhaps at a sporting event, they'll probably be in a different mood from when you meet them in the office or when commuting.

So although our experiences of direct contact with different people may not run to the thousands in terms of individuals, the actual probabilities of other people's moods or "states" influencing yours is massive when you consider how many encounters you have on a day to day basis.

I say all this to reassure you.

I have experienced these hundreds of thousands of meetings with unpredictable human beings and live to tell the tale.

I have survived in the "human jungle" – and so will you.

The point of this is to prove that we cannot avoid contact with other human beings if we are to live a fulfilling life, rich with meaningful activities, fun and happiness – and achieve our goals.

Internal mood may be influenced through other people and change depending on what others say and do when they are in our "orbit".

You can be affected by other people's words and moods and you could literally be all over the place emotionally, at the mercy of those thousands of encounters with unpredictable people during your lifetime.

However, how would it feel if you could interact with people, every day, and not be affected by their words or moods?

Human beings need to interact, they need to be part of a community, enjoy intimacy and work in groups in which each member compliments others.

All this interaction can create stressful situations that affect your emotional state.

However, stress in itself is a good thing, an important defence mechanism, when it's controlled and short term.

Many people are under pressure and sometimes it's easy to pass this pressure on to others, maybe intentionally but generally not, causing them to "catch" stress, almost as if it is a viral infection.

Millions of people every day "catch" stress from others, easier than catching the common cold.

This will often be through a situation at work, where many times stress is "delegated".

It could also be in the family, where members take on stress from others either to share troubles or just through inherent similarities in their genetic blueprints which may by dormant but could be fired off by the very interaction which should be helpful.

Then there are the strangers we meet every day who just stress us out because of what they do and the way they do it which affects our own world.

I have worked with many different types of people and for many different types of bosses.

There's the "need to" boss.

"We need to get this report out tonight"

"We need to work smarter"

"We need to sell twice as many cars this week"

You know the sort. Only the "we" usually happens to be everyone except the boss.

Then there's the "You might like to" boss.

"You might like to stay a little later tonight?"

"You might like to work through lunch today?"

"You might like to see me before you go home?"

Then there's the boss that is just "in your face" all the time. Arriving at your desk unannounced, disrupting your day, pulling you this way and that with conflicting demands and precious little time to respond or react.

There are times I have gone home from the office determined never to set foot in the place again, but then I find myself back there next day, through necessity, and the whole cycle continues.

This can also affect us in school and home situations.

I have worked in some of the more stressful environments but with hindsight I can say that they've been proving grounds for learning techniques that beat stress.

Whatever country you may reside in, stress is evident in all cultures.

This book concentrates on cultural stressors related to the Western situation such as may be found in the United Kingdom or the United States etc. and these cultures have grown out of lifestyle choices influenced by historical events, shaped by attitudes passed down from previous generations.

However, this book is not about reflecting on the past. It's not about how we arrived but where we are - it's about now!

One of the first stress-busting truths on this book is that you do NOT have to go back, you do not need to know why stress affects you, but you need to know how it affects you!

How and now!

So although we know that our history has shaped our culture and attitudes, and consequently the way we interact with each other, it is not important to go there – really!

I will help you beat your stress arising from living in the culture that exists now, which is where you are now.

There are techniques in the exercises that employ some virtual "time travel" but we will certainly not be dwelling on or in the past.

Before we move on, let me explain what I mean by time travel in the context of this book.

Your central nervous system, the brain, the spinal cord – all those bits that make up your "mind" and your awareness of "self" doesn't generally know the difference between a real and a vividly imagined experience.

So when you use your "imagination" or "Reality Simulator" to create images, still or moving, on that screen in your mind, they can be of situations which exist in the present, or can be memories of the past, imaginations of the future, or situations which you have seen on TV or movies or that you have just made up.

The same part of the brain creates memories and imagines future events.

So before the first exercise, I'd just like to briefly mention why I believe we suffer needlessly when we let others stress us out.

You may not feel like it now, but you will be able to separate yourself from people who may cause your stress.

This is because stress can cause us to focus on negative emotions and comments emanating from others.

Eventually you will be able to inwardly smile, even laugh to yourself when you realise how fortunate you are not to be that stress-causing individual.

It really makes little sense to let others stress us out and as we start to perceive the world differently, so we will be able to separate the stress from the person, the person from the stress and say, "there but for the grace of God, go I!"

Break Out!

(Please read the exercise through first. Then to enter into the interactive process ask someone to read it aloud to you slowly in a calm clear voice or for best effect, record it and listen back to enable you to work through it).

Sit in a comfortable position with both feet on the floor.

Close your eyes and go "inside".

Concentrate on your breathing.

Breathe in to the count of 7 and out to the count of 11.

As you breathe out, let go and relax.

Now, imagine your own front door.

What colour is it?

What side is the handle on?

Do you see it as a still or moving image?

Is the image on a screen in front of you or inside your head, or to the side?

Are you watching the image – as if watching a movie?

If you are, you are "disassociated".

Are you "inside" the movie?

If so, then you are "associated".

If you're not sure, in your imagination, reach out and push the door.

Have you gone "inside" the movie yet?

In your mind, notice the hand pushing the door.

Is it your hand?

Look at the detail, closely.

Imagine the hand turning so the palm faces you.

Notice the changing focus as you concentrate on the lines on that hand, the colours and shapes.

Good, you are beginning to associate now.

OK, now pull back away from that hand and just focus on that door again.

You are controlling your internal camera – your mind's eye and you can use this skill to begin to control your reaction to stress triggers such as when you visually recall other people's words or behaviour that negatively affects you.

Open your eyes and come back out and take a few breaths (7/11) and relax.

Now let's try some "time travel".

Close your eyes and focus on that door again.

Imagine the door appears somehow older now. It's wooden, painted, with perhaps a heavy ring-shaped knocker and heavy brass hinges.

This is still your front door, ok?

Notice the lush green ivy around the door or maybe, lilac coloured wisteria clinging to the red bricks surrounding the door.

Look down.

On the step is a neatly wrapped parcel with a bright red ribbon bow.

As you bend to pick it up, notice your gloved hands and the leather cuffs on your woollen coat.

As you lift it to your chest feel the weight of the parcel, shifting the grip to one hand as you reach out to that big brass knocker.

But as you reach forward, the door is opened from the inside.

You are greeted by the sounds of voices, laughing children and music from a string ensemble.

A wonderful smell of wine, brandy, cigar smoke and cooking turkey fills your senses.

A woman facing you, with a flushed but pretty expression of welcome, smiles and beckons you inside.

A roaring fire in a deep hearth beside a full height Christmas tree decorated from floor to ceiling with brightly coloured candles, parcels, baubles and candies.

Take a deep breath and relax.

Open your eyes.

Welcome back.

How does that feel, now?

Congratulations, you have "time travelled" to Christmas 1910!

Were you alive in 1910? If not, where did this image come from?

How did your mind generate this image if it's not a true memory?

Maybe you pieced it together from memories of real events or TV or moves or books. Whatever you did, it is unique to you.

This is your creation. You create what you instruct your brain to create.

Just because it was "imaginary" does that make it any different from a "real" event?

Think about it for a moment.

Once a "real" event has passed, once that moment has gone, it no longer exists as anything other than a collection of chemical reactions inside your Reality Simulator.

You can re-create that past event in your imagination, but so can you create an event that has not happened and you can experience it as being just as real.

And if you add some sounds, some smells and some feelings then it is ever more real.

You can create, watch and then drift into any situation you wish.

And although you may not understand yet why, this will be one major key to beating stress.

Ok, now think of something completely different for a few seconds to "re-boot" and clear your mind.

Now let me take you back to the theme of this chapter, which you were reading before you tripped back to 1910!

The exercises in this book have been created, utilised, experienced and tested and no doubt you will find at least one that will enable you to beat the stress that has led you to this book at this time and place.

The second stress-busting fact you need to be reminded of this this:

It is within your mind that stressful situations are played out, no one else's – yours!

There is one moment, one almost immeasurable moment, when you are actually interacting with your stressor.

Other than that, you are either simulating a future event by anticipating what might happen or you are simulating a past event by reflecting on what has happened.

And here's another truth that will bust the stress myth wide open – you are not a prophet, nor do you have a photographic memory.

What you anticipate or simulate will NOT happen exactly as you expect.

What you remember or simulate did NOT happen exactly as you recall.

And you can change your internal re-presentation of both past and future to suit you and thereby "unhook" any stress which may be attached to it and change your body's emotional response.

It's your mind and therefore it's your show, your deal and your life.

And it's about to get a whole lot better!

I would like to say something about the way the body creates a stress reaction.

As you have been reading these words, relating the situations to your own, you may have noticed a tightening of the stomach muscles or your mind generating "flashback" simulations?

This is your emotional reaction arising from you personalising the generalities I am setting out.

The human mind learns in generalities, which enables us all to take general principles and apply them to our own situation, and thus learn from other people's experiences and mistakes.

Notice that as you read, your mind converts the words to images, perhaps movies, in your mind?

Your incredible brain is personalising my words and re-creating a dream like scenario from snippets of memories on the screen of your mind.

Break Out!

Think of the following word:

Sausage

Do you "see" the word or do you see a sausage?

What is your sausage like? Raw or cooked? Is it barbequed or in a hot dog roll?

Tree

Do you see the word or an image?

What is your tree like?

Is it a tree you know? Is it one from your garden or a nearby park? Is it mature or a young tree? Is it in bloom or in winter, of fall?

Sky

You may by now be seeing an image every time.

There are not a lot of "skies" are there? So you are probably imagining the same sky as anyone else would. However, your sky could be blue or cloudy or dark or and stormy and so on.

You see, not only does your mind probably convert a word to an image; it will probably be a different image for every person on the planet!

The point of this is to show that we all have a different perception and consequently, a different point of view.

One man's stressor is another man's challenge.

So now take some time out now to write down your stressors.

Break Out!

Divide a sheet of plain paper in two.

On the left-hand side write down 6 stressors – those times and events that make your stomach churn, your head spin or your pulse quicken.

For each stressor think of an image or scene that represents the event. Give it a title – such as "Boss" or "Neighbour's Dog" etc.

Now on the right hand side write down 6 instances when you felt extremely relaxed, calm or in control. They can be real or imagined because your central nervous system cannot tell the difference between a real and a vividly imagined event. Think of an image or scene that represents that event and give them a title such as "Holiday" or "Warm Bath" etc.

Be creative and have some fun.

You will learn that there are no limits to the creativity of new perspectives that can occur in your new life.

Next, take one of the stressors you've listed and imagine the scene as if you were watching it on a screen in your mind.

Take the first stress situation now.

When you imagine the scene, notice where the image is located in your field of vision. Is it in front, to the side or inside your head? Is it still or moving? Is it colour or black and white?

If it's moving, make a still or freeze frame and notice how your feelings change.

If it's colour, make it black and white and again notice your feelings.

Return it to its original position and place it to one side, and clear your mind.

Now take one of the calm events you've noted on the right side of the page.

Imagine it now.

Where is the image?

Is it still or moving?

Is it colour or black and white?

If it's still, make it into a lifelike movie.

If it's black and white give it loads of colour.

Make it bigger, brighter and notice how your feelings may change.

Now put that to one side in your mind.

This exercise is to help you gain control over your visual images – make the stress ones less stressful and the calm ones more enjoyable.

So you now have two images – the stressor and the calm image and you have control over both.

OK, now bring back the stress image so that it's in a comfortable location for you in your mind's eye.

Take that stress image and turn it into a black and white still picture and, as if it's on a TV screen, use an imaginary remote control to simply turn it off, just blank it out and watch the image on the screen fade and turn black.

Now quickly switch that TV on again but this time quickly bring the calm image up instead to replace the old one, snap it into exactly the same place in your mind and make it twice as big and twice as colourful.

Now enter into it, drift into it so that you are full immersed in that situation.

How does that feel?

Now think about the old stress image.

How does that feel now?

You should feel a lot calmer when you recall it.

If not, do the exercise again. Quickly swish the black and white stress image with a full colour calm image and make it bright and colourful and enter into it.

Do this with each stressor once a day.

This is one way to help you move from stress, to success!

The Power of Perspective

The techniques in this book will help you utilise the resources you already possess and custom design and install new "software programmes" for your mind, your internal environment, which will naturally interface with the "primary operating system" of the world and the universe which is your external environment.

It will also "download" appropriate parts of the "owner's manual", which is probably something you've never really had proper access to up to now possibly as a result of the educational system in the Western world which runs on very established and restrictive tracks.

You can, and will, be happy, productive, confidant, powerful, relaxed, in control of yourself and your life.

Think for a moment about the nature of what we generally refer to as our "mind".

It's generally understood that we have a conscious mind and an unconscious mind. For the purpose of this book, I'm going with that as a given.

The conscious mind enables us to interface with the environment around us through our senses, the primary senses being those of seeing, hearing, tasting, smelling and touching.

Because 80% of our interaction with the external environment is through senses connected with areas of the face we tend to associate our centre of being, our core self, with the face and head.

If we take a normal 24-hour day, our conscious mind is fully "aware" for about 50 – 75% of that time. For the rest we are "asleep" during which time the conscious mind operates in a different mode.

The conscious mind operates in various modes during a 24-hour period.

We will be fully aware for that 50-75% but our awareness may be affected by dips in concentration when we will feel low or tired and perhaps begin to daydream or trance out.

Like all warm-blooded mammals, we need to eat and sleep during our 24 hours to maintain energy and to enable the body to rejuvenate.

We also need time to assimilate what we've learned during then waking hours and part of this process is linked to the dream state.

The unconscious mind, however, does not sleep. It's active 24/7. Otherwise how would you continue to breathe while you slept?

How would you dream if there was nothing generating the images you recall sometimes when you awake?

How would you wake up?

How would you know that your bladder was full and you needed to get up to pee?

The unconscious mind is like the national power grid. It's always running, supplying us with internal power, energy and light.

But is that unconscious mind, that "core" locked in your head?

We all tend to assume it is.

It's behind our eyes.

Isn't it?

Break Out!

(Read and understand all exercises before attempting them. Remember, work with a partner or record and play back so that you can do the exercise with your eyes closed)

Stand with your legs apart, shoulders back breathe calmly in through the nose, out through the mouth.

Imagine your favourite colour as a glowing gemstone located in the centre of your forehead.

Make it spin and make it glow brighter, place all your awareness right there.

Bunch the fingers of your preferred hand and place them just an inch away from a place in the centre of your forehead.

Concentrate on the energy of your mind being captured in that coloured spinning gemstone.

Imagine you have captured and are holding that gemstone in your bunched fingers.

Now run your fingers down, tracing the outline of your face and body to a position about an inch below your tummy button.

Release the gemstone and imagine it spinning into a position about an inch inside your body.

That can now become the centre of your consciousness.

Notice the difference as your centre of attention has moved from your head to your centre of gravity, the actual centre of your being.

Your Core Self. Open your eyes and return.

As you begin to unlock the power of your unconscious mind your perspective will shift. You will start to appreciate that there is that Core Self, a part of you that is constant, untouchable and pure, and not necessarily located behind your eyes!

By enabling yourself to perceive and understand your life situation from this perspective you can become like the Captain of a ship, observing all that goes on from the bridge of the vessel.

You will be able to keep your personal ship steady as you travel through uncharted, stormy water of life.

Remember, the Captain is always aware, always checking with the engine room that the ship has sufficient energy and power to complete its journey.

Another technique that can help to change your perspective and reframe your world view when things get too "Black and white" or you can't see the wood for the trees is "Stepping Back".

Break Out!

Find a smooth pebble or rock and hold it an inch from your face at eye level and allow your eyes to focus on it.

Then gradually withdraw the rock away from your face and allow your eyes to take in objects surrounding the rock as it moves away from your eyes – objects that are in your peripheral vision will begin to come into view. As you move the rock further from your face your eyes will notice more and more of the surroundings until, when the rock is about 12 inches from your face you may find it just as comfortable to focus on the surroundings as the rock itself.

You are now seeing a bigger picture. You are seeing the rock in the context of its surroundings. You can look at the rock, or you can look at other objects. You can also decide if you want to view the rock from different angles, or perspectives such as from the top, side or from underneath.

You have the ability now to assess the rock for what it really is and the potentials and limitations it offers as an object, or resource.

Instead of having to struggle to focus on the object that obscures your peripheral vision occluding your view and taking up your whole perspective, you now have control over that object and can utilise it to your advantage.

This metaphor illustrates the importance of being able to step back and see the bigger picture when stress has you in its grip.

When the stressor seems to be right in your face, obscuring the view and cutting you off from potential options, ways around the problem, step back.

Another technique for stepping back involves the "Watching Self".

The Watching Self is a way of personalising and utilising the mind's amazing resource of self-awareness that is available to you during all of your waking times.

This is the essence of being Human.

This incredible ability, which you can learn and employ just when you need it, enables you to drift in and out of the part of you that interfaces with the world, where your stress originates, and into your core untouchable inner self.

From that position of the "Watcher" you can begin to recognise what stresses you, what really "pushes your buttons" but like watching it from a disassociated position on a TV or movie screen.

Break Out!

As you read this book, imagine slowly and gently floating up and out of your body. Observe yourself below and hover just a few feet above.

Notice the details of the hands of the "you" down there holding the pages or resting on your lap, or desktop. Look at your head from above, the shape and colour of any hair. Notice your shoulders, arms and legs if you can see them.

Then notice the surroundings, the furniture or, if you're outside, the colour of the grass or flowers.

Take in the sounds and scents in the air and appreciate the freedom you might be feeling – freedom from the body of that you down there.

You are strengthening your Watching Self and by utilising this technique you will soon be able to appreciate what it's like to separate your "core" self from the stress when it has attached itself to and is manifesting to your physical body.

Go a step further and float to a point about ten feet above the "you" down there. Now see what you can see and appreciate all the surroundings.

Begin to use your Reality Simulator to go beyond the imagination into visualisation.

Make the colours bright and vivid.

Forget any limitations such as the room, apartment or house you down there are sitting in. You are your core essence and you are free to wander now.

Drift up to fifty feet above the "you" down there.

Notice the surroundings now! See what you see and hear what you hear and appreciate the sense of the breeze on your skin and in your hair.

How does your stress feel now?

When you're ready, float gently back down into your body.

Take a deep breath in, let it go and relax. Close your eyes, count to five and open them.

Quite a trip.

OK, re-orient your mind with a quick re-focus of your attention right now.

At this point I would suggest you take a break from exercises and let your mind work with the reprogramming it has received so far.

The power of perspective is so important, that I have included some further exercises that follow and these will serve to add to your ability to take what is theory and make a real practical difference to your life.

The three following exercises will strengthen your abilities but take your time and return to them when you feel ready.

Break Out!

This next exercise involves attempting to understand another person's perspective and can be carried out alone or in the company of others.

Let's start alone.

Sit in a relaxed position in a chair with your feet on the floor.

Once you have practiced and perfected the technique you might like to try this with eyes closed but for now you know you can visualise so keep your eyes open.

Image sitting in a chair facing you is someone you love and loves you.

In your mind, using your Reality Simulator, re-create them now. Look into their eyes and smile. Notice the details of their face and the colour of their hair.

You can see the rise and fall of their chest as they breathe. There's a pulse in the neck just below one ear. There's a little moisture on the lips.

How are their feet placed on the floor? How do they hold themselves in the seat? What's their posture?

How do you think their clothes feel against their skin and their feet feel in their shoes, if they're wearing any?

Now, gently and slowly drift up and out of your body and into the person opposite.

Like putting on a new suit of clothes, slip into their body.

See what you see and notice how that feels.

Get used to the feel of their body around you and the clothes against your skin.

Run your tongue over strange teeth and taste the lips.

Notice the sensation of the chair or seat holding your body and how your hands feel.

Now look from their perspective into the eyes of "you" opposite.

Feel the love that's transmitting between you.

Begin to appreciate how it feels to be that other person sitting opposite you.

How does that feel, really?

What do you feel about the "you" that you now see?

See yourself with the love of that other person.

Smile.

You smile back.

Gently drift back into your own body.

Take a deep breath in, let that breath out, relax and see that person you love opposite.

Close your eyes, count to five, open them, and relax.

Take a deep breath and relax.

Do the re-boot and get your attention back to the here and now.

Welcome back.

How does that feel, now?

The next exercise involves understanding another person's perspective but who would be a stranger.

You can do this in public or in your imagination. Remember, your Reality Simulator doesn't know the difference between a real or vividly imagined event.

You are on a bus or train. Select a ride that will last at least 10 minutes.

Choose a person sitting opposite and begin to try to understand something about them.

Male or female?

Age?

Married?

Parent?

Student?

What type of work?

Nationality?

Are they active or passive?

Alone or with others?

Why are they travelling today?

Have they come from a stressful meeting?

Are they travelling to a meeting?

Are they worried about what might happen?

Are they worried about their future?

Spend a few minutes assessing what clues they are giving you from the expression, posture, and demeanour.

Now, float out of your body and into the body of that other person.

Take a moment to orient yourself.

What do you see?

Take a look around at the people from this new perspective.

What can you feel, physically?

The warmth of the carriage or bus?

The feeling of the people around, pressing in?

How does that make you feel?

Notice yourself sitting over there.

Smile?

Now begin to appreciate this body's point of view.

Appreciate and sense the internal physiology. The breathing. Taste in the mouth. Run your tongue over strange teeth and lips.

Is there any pain in that body?

Is there any pain in that mind?

What memories might this mind be holding?

Notice how you feel now.

Gently drift back into your own body.

Take a deep breath, hold it, let it go and relax.

Close your eyes, count to five, open them.

Do the reboot; get your attention back now.

The final exercise in this section is to utilise the floatation technique in a situation that you know will be stressful.

This will be a meeting with more than you and one other person present.

Imagine a situation such as a business meeting, school situation, resident's meeting, sales seminar, any situation you have experienced which you found stressful.

It would be really good to use a recent event where you may be able to recall conversations and words spoken that may have affected you adversely in some way.

Imagine the situation now.

Use that Reality Stimulator to fully recreate the situation.

Notice the room, the furniture, the floor covering, and the ceiling.

Notice the windows and what you can see beyond them.

Is it warm or cold?

How does your tummy feel inside?

Do you have a slight headache?

Is there a little sheen of sweat on your top lip?

Is your mouth dry?

Look around at the people assembled in the room.

Use your new skills to assess them and select one or two, particularly those who would be your antagonists, and begin to allow your perspective to shift to one particular person of your choosing.

Now gently float out of your body and into the body of that other person.

Take a moment to get your bearings.

Look around the room and see yourself over there.

Do you feel like smiling?

Now you need to undertake a feelings audit of your new body and mind.

Physical

External

Internal

Teeth

Lips

Taste

Heartbeat

Breathing

Eyesight

Any aches or pains?

Now begin to allow your imagination to scan that new body and mind's internal agendas and motivations.

Recall the purpose of the meeting.

What might be this person's agenda?

What do they want or need to achieve from this?

How important is it to them?

As you go through this process, look into the eyes of the you over there.

Feel the love and respect emanating from you over there.

Now drift gently back into your own body.

Breathe deeply, let it go, close your eyes, count to five, open them and relax.

Take a deep breath and relax.

Open your eyes.

Do the re-boot.

Welcome back.

How does that feel, now?

It's not just visualisation, it's using the full power of the Reality Simulator to create an environment or landscape, preview yourself living within it, then downloading and install it as your future.

Architects do it when then create a building from their imagination and what's more concrete than a building?

Business does it when it creates a strategic plan that then becomes reality over an agreed timescale and products or services manifest from thoughts!

There is nothing on this earth, which is not part of nature, that didn't start out as a human thought.

Our minds create our reality.

That's another way to help you move from stress to success.

Stress and Your Body

For managing stress it is good to get a basic understanding of how the brain manifests stress in the body and how we can react to stressors.

The techniques in this book are not based on the traditional concepts of willpower, self-denial or positive thinking.

They utilise natural learning methods which overwrite patterns that have caused you stress in the past.

Go with it and you'll find those old perceptions changing.

The human mind generalises as a learning principle and this applies in terms of learning useful patterns of behaviour for doing repetitive tasks.

For example, we learn how to open a door.

We turn the handle and push.

Then we have a general understanding or template that we can apply to the external environment, particularly in terms of doors.

If we come across a door that opens inwards, or slides sideways, then we have to learn an additional template that serves to increase our knowledge base regarding doors.

We tend not to forget the first principle but we now add additional information to our "doors knowledge base".

We have the generalisation regarding doors, but we also have the understanding that there is more than one type of door.

We have a generalisation principle.

Similarly we also learn to recognise painful events so that we learn not to do them again and therefore not to suffer such pain again.

Such an example would be stubbing our toe.

We experience pain from this event and we have a new learning principle. We have a specific event that generalises into the pattern that stubbing the toe creates pain. However, we also have the potential to do it again so we become more careful. It doesn't stop us from walking; it just makes us more careful.

It is said that 90-95% of problems in our lives stem from stress.

That's a huge amount of grief that we don't need to suffer. So how can we learn to think more effectively and take control of stress situations?

One key element is in the way the brain changes modes during waking and sleeping states.

There is the learning sleep mode known as REM (Rapid Eye Movement) state, which is when the brain is active but the brain creates a cataleptic state in the body and effectively glues the eyelids closed. However, the eyes are moving rapidly from side to side beneath those closed lids. The brain creates an internally generated dreamscape from bits of memories and stuff you may have seen on TV before you went to bed within which you act out un-discharged emotional situations from the day.

It does not require stimulus from the external environment, nor does it require you to interface with the external environment through your senses.

That internally generated reality fades as we awake and the sensory external environment kicks in, overlaying the dreamscape that is generally soon forgotten.

When we are dreaming, the reality simulated by our Reality Simulator, can feel like a credible experience. It's only upon waking that it fades in comparison with "real" life's predictable patterns.

During REM, we are laying down new templates. New learning is being set in place.

So changing brainwave patterns via access of

REM state is hugely beneficial, not only in sleep but also in trance states such as therapeutic hypnosis.

In therapeutic hypnosis we are effectively recreating the natural learning REM state that happens in sleep.

The brain has two hemispheres and the left hemisphere is the most dominant and logical side active at the peaks of sleep mode, and the right side is active in REM state for 15/20 out of every 90 minutes in sleep time.

To maintain healthy balance we need to allow ourselves 15-20 minutes REM at times every day during the day. This is clearly not easy to achieve for a lot of people in the busy lives we lead.

Hypnosis, be it through self-induction, listening to a recording or with a therapist can assist in entering the REM for a brief period such as 20 minutes.

Recent technological advances have enabled the mapping of neurotransmitters in the brain that chemically underpin of the way we feel.

These neurotransmitters release chemicals such as endorphins or serotonin that create feelings of wellbeing and happiness.

The way we think and feel influences the

functions of our bodies.

The immune system functions more efficiently when we are happy.

The entire nervous system operates more effectively when we are relaxed.

The mind therefore, in relaxation, persuades the body.

Remember, the mind does not know the difference between a real and vividly imagined event.

The mind is effectively a "Reality Simulator".

The body listens to every word that the brain tells it

So an example would be like when we blush when remembering something embarrassing the body reacts or responds to relaxing stimulation.

The brain controls the body, producing endorphins, produces relaxation, produces the opposite of the stress we experience every day

In the brain, responding to an external or imagined stimulus, the amygdala alerts the adrenals.

But in terms of stress, the brain doesn't know the difference between a man holding a knife to our throat or our inability to pay the rent and thus be faced with eviction from our home – it's the same stress reaction.

We are built to cope with stress in the short term, but not over the long term, such as prolonged anxiety about home or job loss, and that will take its toll on the body.

More stress in life means that the brain will require more REM time which usually takes place at night and that REM activity can be very active as the stressful situations have to be played out in dreamscapes during the night and thus the person receives less rest and feels exhausted in the morning, even though they may have been in bed for longer than usual.

Stressors are the external environmental stimuli, or anchors, which kick off the stress reaction in you.

How do you respond to them?

If you don't respond then it's not acting upon you, and it has no control over you.

Generally, the stressor will trigger an emotion deep inside, that emotion starts in the brain and it hits your central nervous system faster than the speed of thought – literally.

That's why it's not thoughts that create emotion but it is the emotion that creates the thought.

The base primordial part of the brain, not the more comparatively recent neo-cortex, that larger part of the brain, is where the emotion kicks in and the thought, which is the human's response to the reaction, comes later.

The thought comes through the neo-cortex which reasons, judges, calculates and considers the response to the emotion. And because humans are more advanced than other mammals, that time of consideration enables us to consider the consequences of any actions we may take as a result of the emotion.

However, when we are in the height of emotional response – perhaps we could refer to this as "emotional hijack" – the higher brain does not function, it is over-ridden by the emotional brain which is protecting the human by putting it on survival alert.

So "road rage" or "red mist" or whatever you may refer to as that time when you just can't think straight but just want to do something stupid to the person who's upset you is caused by that emotional hijack.

Have you ever been in a tense situation, a confrontation of some form, and it's only after the event that you begin to think about what you could or should have done to handle the situation differently or in a better way?

It's anything from a minute to perhaps ten minutes before the mist clears and you can begin to think logically again.

You have literally lost the ability to reason.

Your brain has put you into alert mode and you have to learn to focus, relax and allow that to dissipate.

Fear is real; now, it's the brain's response to an event happening right now.

Anxiety is in the imagination, possible, future, an event that may never happen.

Anxiety is when we imagine something may be happening; it's faulty use of the imagination. The reality simulator of your mind is creating a "What if" scenario which it then reacts to by panicking! How crazy is that?

But remember, especially when faced with a "what if" or emotional hijack that just about anything that can happen to anyone has happened to someone at some time or another. You are not the first and certainly not the last.

So the process you experience with emotional hijack goes something like this:

The stressor kicks off the alert in the brain and you get freeze first, like a rabbit in car headlights or a mouse when faced with a cat – and like a human just about to be eaten by a lion.

Your eyes can move – because you need to scan the environment for an escape route.

You sweat – because that releases pungent, unpleasant smells and when dry makes your hands sticky so it's easier for you to climb.

Your breathing speeds up – ready to fight or run.

Your pulse and heart rate increase - ready to fight or run.

You might just vomit – so you're not quite so tasty a meal!

Your symptoms are the same as when you have a panic attack as a result of some traumatic event. This is the same response as asking a question such as am I going to die, am I going to be humiliated?

Panic attacks can be as real as a reaction to the actual event.

This is because the memory of the event has got stuck in a part of the brain that does not allow the memory to dissipate as with normal memories (Amygdala). It stays very real and immediate so you can end up re-living the event over and over and each time the memory is just as vivid.

Worse still stressors that are not exactly the same

as the original event can trigger the memory. This is the brain's learning pattern of generalisation but working in a negative way. It is a sloppy match to the learned template, which is there to protect you but is working overtime.

It's a bit like a faulty car alarm, going off at the slightest noise or touch. It needs re-setting!

An example of such a situation follows:

One Friday morning, a girl (let's call her Monica) was travelling to work on the London underground train service – the "tube" as it is known. The Tube is always most crowded at the places where the trains enter central London.

Monica had travelled in from one of the stations a few stops outside of London so she was able to get a seat. The seat she occupied was one that backed onto the windows in the side of the train and faced into the carriage. There is a similar row of seats opposite.

Gradually the carriage filled with people who had to stand between the seat she was occupying and the ones opposite.

As the carriage became more crowded, people were standing with their backs to Monica, tight against her legs.

She began to feel quite claustrophobic as she was

sitting and those standing were much taller and overbearing.

Then suddenly all the lights went out and the train suddenly screeched to a halt and people were thrown about.

Monica, along with many other people in the carriage, screamed.

The darkness, the sweaty smell of the commuters, the suddenness of the event, the fear of the unknown and the brain's kicking into "alert" mode all added up to create an anchor in her mind.

She had learned a new template, although she was unaware of it at that time.

Fortunately the stop was temporary and the power was soon back on and the train was on its way.

The following Saturday evening, Monica was at a party she had been invited to at a friend's flat.

She was sitting on a couch, chatting to some friends sitting either side of her. After a while, having been totally absorbed in the chat, she decided to get up to fix a drink.

She faced front to find that the room was full of people and they were standing right in front of her, just as if she were in a crowded tube train.

Suddenly the lights were dimmed and she suffered a panic attack.

Instantly she was back on that tube train and the memory triggered the brain's alert response.

She screamed and people looked around at her.

She felt foolish, but more importantly, she later needed to rehearse the trigger event under therapeutic hypnotic conditions for the memory to be dissipated and for her not to suffer the response again.

Such is the power of the learning process, whether for good or bad, gain or pain.

But also that learning process can be re-programmed in safe hypnotic therapeutic situations that engage the same natural learning process as REM sleep.

Sloppy "pattern matching" can also lead potentially to a phobia, such as fear of spiders.

It's ok to be aware of the scuttling of a spider, suddenly across your path or in a dimly lit room. However, many people actually have a phobic fear of spiders. This is the old "car alarm" going off just a bit too freely.

Think of fear as a pet dog!

The dog barks to warn you that there may be an intruder in the house –and that's good

But if the dog barks at everyone – that's not good

Fear looks to me as giving it a lead so if I'm able to reassure it that all is well then it will settle down.

In hypnotherapy, we can take a link out of a chain of events that may trigger a phobic or faulty alert response.

Like the domino effect – if we take out one, the whole system cannot continue the process.

Some useful stress busters are:

1. Use a relaxed state, trance or hypnosis to enable the brain to kick off the REM state and "rehearse" the situation using your Reality Simulator. You can access a good time and "anchor" that good feeling by pinching your thumb and finger together and then reproduce it later and apply it to a stressful scenario.
2. Chew gum. Ever seen a stressed cow?
3. Do something normal such as 7/11 breathing which tells your fear instinct that nothing very abnormal is happening so it returns the body to normal operating state.
4. Grade the situation from 1-10 as this introduces shades of grey and introduces the ability to rationalise and analyse, then re-grade later
5. Use the Watching Self.

What also happens when your brain kicks off the alert response is this:

The adrenal glands go into overdrive, releasing adrenaline that takes a few minutes to dissipate into your system.

The digestive system shuts down (you don't need to eat a sandwich while being chased by a tiger!)

Blood is diverted to muscles and blood pressure increases to pump us up, ready to fight or run.

Pupils dilate (to focus attention).

Sex drive shuts down (pretty clearly you are not likely to make love to the tiger that's attacking you!)

After 2-3 minutes with no outcome from the stressor, the body can return to normal state.

But it's the longer-term effects that cause real problems.

But the longer-term response produces cortisol and digestive problems result because the blood flow is being diverted away to the muscles

The immune system works less hard

Growth / healing hormones are compromised

Higher thought processes switch off (that's the neo-cortex).

The body re-routes resources to appropriate areas when different external stimulus activates a response.

Cortisol steals glucose from the hippocampus – the memory module of the brain, so the memory is stuck in the amygdala.

So stress directly manifests in the body.

Attitudes to events in our lives have an impact on the body's defence systems

In 1920 Pavlov undertook his famous experiment with dogs where he programmed them to salivate in the expectation of food when he rang a bell. In the same, but clearly more complex principles, the human immune system is conditioned by experience, either real or vividly imagined.

The healing response of the immune is a rich system of mind and body connections.

Thoughts and feelings play an important part in our physical health so it's important to be in control and manage them well.

Hormones produced under stress can impair the immune function.

Emotional reactions can impair the function of organs.

Emotional attitudes (or traits) could double the risk of a range of diseases.

Harboured attitudes, guilt, bitterness, grudges can really screw with your emotions and consequently produce a stream of thoughts which need to be dealt with in the waking or sleeping state.

It's a vicious cycle which is fuelled by and in turn produces emotions based around anxiety, grief, tension, hostility, suspicion and pessimism that in turn can increase the chances of headaches, heart disease, ulcers, asthma, arthritis and skin disorders

Excessive anxiety compromises the immune system leading to possibilities of viral infection, plaque formation, blood clotting, diabetes, irritable bowel syndrome, bowel disease, hippocampus & memory disorder and even cancer.

It reduces the body's ability to fight diseases and infections and eventually could lead to colds, herpes, of if infected, HIV related symptoms

There can also be a poorer response to vaccines and wounds heal slower

Brief bursts of stress, producing the flight or fight response are ok but if the energy generated is not expended in appropriate physical action or dispersed the chemical cocktail and on-going physical arousal weakens the immune system.

If your body is geared up to either fight or run, what's the best way to disperse that pent up tension? Fight or run! If you can't fight, then go for a run!

Not only is running and exercise good for the stress relief it also releases endorphins, the brain's "happy chemicals", so have you got a double benefit.

It's important to have a sense of well being and ability to cope, have an element of control over life.

For some, stress is, however, a coping mechanism itself.

It is vital to understand the link between emotions and bodily manifestations.

The heart gets hurt when people allow themselves to be made angry.

Being angry kicks off the flight or fight response as quickly as anxiety does.

Stress hormones are released.

Heart rate rises.

Blood pressure rises.

Cholesterol level rises.

Anger, hostility or jealousy can be causes of this.

Hostility ties in with isolation / lack of connection with the wider community.

Also *"PERCEIVED OWNERSHIP"* can stretch your stress boundaries.

For example, people refer to;

My wife

My house

My property

My job

My car

My family

My community

My church

All these perceptions of control or ownership can create overblown responsibility and can create personal ties and that's a lot of territory to defend.

This is actually egocentric.

Challenges to the "owned" things leads to anxiety reactions of protectiveness and fear of potential loss.

We need to loosen ties, so that we are not affected when things happen in these areas.

This all affects the brain and the heart and manifests in disease of the body.

Break Out!

This is an exercise using a technique known as "anchoring". It is best undertaken in a full therapeutic hypnotic situation but even when undertaken less intensely through playback or perhaps with a friend who may be able to help you, it will greatly benefit your ability to utilise the resources you have within you from your own life's experience.

Sit in a comfortable position with both feet on the floor.

Close your eyes and go "inside".

Take a deep breath in and as you breathe out, let go and relax.

As you go down, breathe deeply, holding your in breath to a count of 7 and then breathing slowly out to a count of 11.

Notice how, after you've expelled all the air from your lungs, the in- breath happens all by itself and then allow your breathing to deepen.

Imagine wandering down a winding pathway in some woods or by a river.

Just relax and let go as you notice the feeling of the path beneath your feet and the scents in the air and the little changes in the breeze on your skin.

As you go deeper down this path, in your mind, count down from 10 to 1.

When you reach the number 1, you will find yourself by a doorway or an opening that arouses your curiosity.

Go through the doorway or opening and find yourself in a wonderful, special place of your choosing.

It might be somewhere from your past, a very happy time of your youth, or it might be a place from a holiday or even from a book or film.

As you relax in this place, allow your mind to bring to your attention a time when you felt really calm, happy and in complete control of your situation.

Really enter into that now.

See what you see and hear what you hear and fully immerse yourself so you can feel how you felt at that time.

Now take those feelings and double them in intensity. Really feel good.

Now press the thumb and forefinger of your right hand together.

Keep pressing as you once again double the intensity of those feelings of being in control and calm and relaxed.

Relax you fingers now.

As you relax deeper, allow your mind to transport you to a future time when you will be facing a situation that you know will be stressful. It may be an exam, a test, a new job, a meeting – whatever comes to mind.

Once you begin to be aware of rising tension in your emotions, press your thumb and finger together and get back that feeling of relaxed calm and control.

Notice how differently you respond to that stressful situation.

You might be more confident, more at ease and in control.

Fully enter the situation and see through your eyes and hear through your ears and make the feelings stronger.

Notice how you are relaxed in that situation.

OK now bring those feelings of relaxed, calm control

back with you as you head back through the doorway or opening, up the path as you count back from 1 to 10.

Take a deep breath and let it go.

Open your eyes and relax.

OK, re-orient your mind with a quick re-focus of your attention right now.

Notice how it feels now when you think of that potentially stressful situation?

If you rehearse this, you will introduce new patterns into your unconscious mind.

Also try scaling such feelings from 1-10 before and after any of the exercises you undertake.

This will help you understand what works best in your situation because we are all different in the way we perceive and interface with our external environment.

Purpose, Meaning, Goals

It is important to have goals in your life.

If you have a clear goal, then all that you do can be a strategic part of achieving that goal.

If you do not have a clearly identified goal that you are working towards, you can end up being at the mercy of other people's goals and agendas.

Are there people in "orbit" around you who have their own individual goals clearly defined and could just be using you to meet their needs.

Would you rather be in control?

Wouldn't it be better to be able to resist a stronger person's persuasiveness by simply being able to stick to your own goals?

For example, you may want to go and buy a new car but a person in your orbit who has their own agenda for, perhaps, wanting to have the best car in the group so they will try to influence your decision.

Represent on a large piece of paper all the people you have regular contact with as a universe with you at the centre and around you orbiting solar systems for family, friends and colleagues – you could base this on the illustration below.

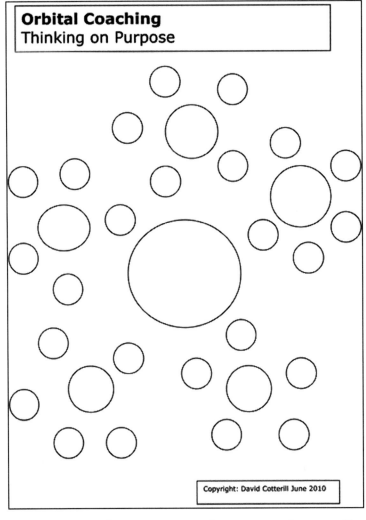

Orbital Coaching
Thinking on Purpose

Copyright: David Cotterill June 2010

We all have a close group of contacts in our lives at during any given period.

This may depend on where we live or how we socialise but can also be influenced by the sort of work we do.

1: *Family*

Family can have a very strong influence on our lives.

There is our immediate family – parents, brothers, sisters and offspring such as sons or daughters.

Then there are the more distant relatives such as in-laws, grandparents or grandchildren.

There are also the slightly more distant relatives.

Use the Orbital illustration as a template to map out your family members who are in your orbit.

The family can have a strong influence on your direction in life and consequently your stress levels if their goals do not match yours or you have not settled on a clear direction yourself.

Parents can try to influence you, in many cases seeing you as the route to some form of success that they failed to achieve or adversely, planting some form of negative suggestion early in life which either restricts your growth ("you'll never be any good") or inspires you to become driven by the desire to prove them wrong.

A driven desire to prove parents wrong can be an incredibly strong motivator but it can lead to immense stress because you are always living to someone else's expectations which may not be clarified.

I've known people who have continued to be driven by parental challenge long after their parents have died.

A spouse or partner can act in a similar way as a motivator / stressor in the same way on many occasions.

If you have a clear goal in life when you meet your partner or spouse they will tend to accept that as part of the package, an integral part of you. However if you find a goal or direction later, that can cause additional stress if the partner is not signed up to the same goal.

Further stress comes with family commitments.

As a parent, you may have to share your time between your own goals and motivators and those of your offspring.

It is not always healthy to impose your value upon your offspring during their latter informative years (11-16), as they will be forming their own value system and beginning to experiment and reach out further in their life experience.

You will need to find a balance between your goals and assisting them in meeting theirs in a guiding and understanding manner.

The more distant relatives can also have an influencing effect if you do not have clear goals and purpose.

For example, a particularly strong and influential family member can take up much of your leisure time if they view this as "spare" time. You could end up helping them with their latest ventures, helping them move home, going out to see a car they've got their eye on over the weekend and even be dragged off to sports events.

Many people find it stressful simply saying no, particularly when the other person is very influential or persuasive or may even feign hurt when a refusal is received.

So if you have a clear goal in your life, even if you make it known to the family or not, you are able to dictate the agenda.

It's not as if you have to become a self-centred individual who simply refuses to help anyone else. It's just that if others know you have things to do on weekends they are going to be less offended if you choose to say no if they request help.

Similarly, once you have gone through the painful process of sitting down with parents and explaining that your life goals may not exactly meet with their expectations for your life, then the chances are they will understand in the future.

As with any such situation, it is always useful to consider the other person's perspective.

Are your parents likely to be deeply hurt when you tell them you no longer want to be a train driver or an airline pilot?

If you don't understand them, do some visualisation and slip into their lives for a little while.

Maybe do some time travel and try to get their perspective on why they have such expectations for your life, if that is the case.

Furthermore, you can do this for any other member of your family as well.

Try to get "under their skin" through visualisation and floatation.

These are the techniques you have practised in earlier modules in the book.

Not only will this help you understand your family, you will begin to identify social structures, motivators and types.

You may also begin to really start to get an overview on family culture and how it affects attitudes.

Think about the solar system of your family now.

See if you can identify the stronger characters.

Are there any real manipulators?

Identify the influences, the motivators, and cultural attitudes and then see if you can construct a strategy to begin to influence them.

2: *Friends and acquaintances*

I had a friend who assumed that I always wanted to do what he wanted to do.

I had to go to sports events with him to watch his team. Even worse, I generally had to drive!

He assumed my kids wanted to watch the same events that his kids did.

The stress was passed down the family line! Through my weakness and inability to say no, they had to endure sitting through hours of sports and events that they really didn't want to.

It was also assumed that my family would want to spend all day Sunday at their house.

Of course the trouble with this is that they were comfortable in their own home but we were the guests and however they tried to reassure us that we could "make ourselves at home" it's just not that easy in someone else's house.

Now, if I had identified my own clear goals and agenda at that time, it would have been so much easier to be able to say no.

I would not be saying no just because I didn't want to spend Sunday at his house, I would have been able to do so with a clear conscience and that I wasn't hurting his feelings.

It's not that I was weak, but when I think about it now, it was a real waste of valuable time because we could have enjoyed a really nice lunch or dinner together perhaps once or twice a year, rather than getting frustrated sitting in someone else's dining room for hours on end, week after week.

Think about the solar system of your friends now. Use the template.

See if you can identify the stronger characters.

Are there any real manipulators?

Identify the influences, the motivators, and the cultural attitudes and then see if you can construct a strategy to begin to influence them.

3: *Work colleagues & bosses*

Maybe your greatest stressor is your immediate boss?

It's just as likely your stress could come from that colleague who seems to have it in for you all the time?

Or even that colleague who always seems to have something better than you?

Then there's that colleague that you have to manage and who just won't do what you want them to do. You just can't believe why they work for the company when it's quite obvious that they don't want to make any effort.

By the end of this chapter, by using the template and the exercises, you will have a clear idea of your goals and a strategy to ensure that those in your orbit will be aware of them

You will be in a stronger position, you will be able to influence others and even recruit them to assist you to meet your goals.

Meaning and purpose is vital to the healthy mind-set of a human being.

It is a basic need for all individuals.

Do you ever wake up thinking "why?"

Why am I here?

Why was I born here?

Why did I end up here?

Do you wake up thinking, "What is the purpose of my life?"

You need to be so careful of wandering thoughts on such topics!

I expect if you were to think reasonably and in a structured way for a little while you would grasp some basic meanings to your existence.

We don't have to have all the answers to the meaning of life to enable us to get out of bed in the morning, but it's good to make a start with a simple exercise.

Break Out!

Who are you responsible for?

Do you have any dependants?

Kids?

Partner?

Cat?

Parrot?

Mouse, rat or gerbil?

Count anyone or anything that is alive.

What would happen to them if you weren't around tomorrow?

If that gives you a little shudder of emotion or guilt, then good, because you have some sense of responsibility and therefore you have identified the first reason, the first purpose, the first meaning to your life at the present moment, in your present orbit.

You don't have to understand what makes the universe tick to know that you have a sense of responsibility built into you. Maybe it's tucked away a little deeper down that it might be. Perhaps that is a sign of the slight feeling of depression you may be experiencing at the moment.

But the start of change comes with the smallest shift of perception.

Think about this. If the reason you have to get out of bed is to feed that little furry friend, then you have identified one of the most basic human qualities – compassion!

Can you add any other dependants to your "reason for being" list?

Many of you will find that as you consider your list of dependents, the stress levels will begin to rise because those dependents will not all be small and furry!

Some might be in their teen years and not at all small and hardly furry at all!

Some might be at the end of their lives, having given their all to enable you to grow and have opportunities in life and now you are perhaps feeling that you are forced to care for them.

Think about that. Don't you owe it to them?

Meaning and purpose can arise from the need to care for others.

Take yourself out of the picture.

Visualise what would happen if you didn't turn up when they expected you?

What would they do?

What would you do if you were them?

Now make some contingency plans in case you don't turn up one day.

Go back to those orbiting families, friends and work colleagues. How can you involve them in your situation?

It will reduce your underlying stress if you know you have others you can rely on to care for your dependents, even for a short time, if you're unable to make it.

But maybe you can't identify any dependents?

So, maybe you're not in a position to care for any small and furries at the moment?

Let's try to identify another meaning for your life.

Break Out!

Imagine this.

You wake up tomorrow morning and you seem to be the only person alive in your town, or village or city.

So do you go back to bed?

Its ok, you say to yourself, I have no dependents – furry or otherwise – so it really doesn't matter if I just stay in bed all day. At least no-one's going to disturb me!

But if you really stop and think about it, there maybe is something niggling at the back of your mind.

You are a human being, right?

Visualise this situation.

Deserted streets, cars abandoned no life at all.

You see a clear blue-sky overhead, a calm breeze on your skin and a citrus scent from the fruit trees along the pathways and the taste of salt from the nearby ocean on your lips.

You sit on a bench and take a deep breath.

You have no dependents, no one to try and contact but maybe you experience a slight twist in the depths of your stomach at the dawning realisation that no one will be trying to contact you either.

In fact, is there actually any real difference between being the last person alive and being a person without dependants?

Stressful though they may be dependents give you purpose and meaning.

Maybe it's time to think about re-establishing contact with someone?

If they're still alive!

OK, take a deep breath, open your eyes and come back.

Think of something completely different to reboot your mind.

One final exercise for this module:

Break Out!

Make a list of the 5 most important people in your life right now.

Make a list of the 5 most important possessions in your life right now.

Make a list of your 5 most important virtues right now.

Make a list of 5 things that DRIVE you right now.

Make a list of 5 goals you have achieved in your life to date.

Now summarise all this into one statement that will become your "mission statement", your meaning and purpose.

Take Control of Your Mind

One of the first and most important steps in getting on top of stress and re-focusing the resources you have to keep in reserve to deal with it is to get the management of your mind back under your own control.

The general education and parenting set up in the western world is adequate to "get us going" as individuals but can leave us seriously wanting in a lot of aspects when we find ourselves interacting with the "real world".

At this stage it will be useful to start to identify factors from your time in education which may have, without you notice, have installed limiting beliefs which have, up to now, affected the way you perceive and operate in the world.

The exercise later in this module will be an opportunity to do this practically, but it is worth reminding ourselves how the education system has served us up to now.

Generally the "education system" will begin through parents or carers during the first 3 or 4 years of your life.

Children are generally taught to learn through methods their parents or carers inherited from their own parents and carers.

By the time they are ready for their first "schooling" experience, children will have an understanding of basic principles but they will generally have been taught in a bit of a vacuum, in the isolation of their immediate family or care circles.

Soon after entering primary schooling, they will begin to pick up the basics of the language of the culture they are in.

Much of this culture will be handed down, such as nursery rhymes and metaphorical stories within which lie wisdom teachings.

These stories contain embedded generalisations and templates that children will need to learn to interpret and apply to their situations as they grow and make their way in the world.

However, whether some of the popular nursery rhymes are completely relevant to the 21st century global community are questionable.

Children are then tested at different stages to assess how they compare with accepted activity and understanding and, if they are generally on track, are considered to be "normal" and so the process continues.

During these early years of general education, the young people are picking up cultural values from friends and other contacts.

They will begin to form opinions that will perhaps be supported and encouraged by others, but it is also likely that their opinions will be frowned upon if they are too radical or not following traditionally accepted guidelines.

Character is formed through such interactions and the child's personality begins to be formed through "rubbing elbows" with others, as well as through the educational system.

Generally, children are educated by way of a relatively "dry" system and many of them report this as being "boring" and this can eventually lead to discontent and rebellion.

Young people soon learn that they have more power in numbers and begin to group together with others of like mind so that they can begin to find ways to manifest their unrest and dissatisfaction with the system.

Through the education system, there are outlets for such frustration, although generally they tend to be played down.

Education is usually monitored through written examinations where children have to prove they have listened and learned by answering questions in a timed situation.

Very little of this education system bears any resemblance to the real lives children live outside of the school or after they leave the system.

It might be only when they leave education, that they realise just how much they still have to learn to enable them to make their way in the world, be it their local community or in the global marketplace.

Recent advances in technology have enabled scientists to more fully understand how the human brain learns, stores and recalls information.

These findings suggest that the type and form of education that has been so popular in western culture only stimulates about one tenth of brain potential.

Until the system catches up and realises just how the brain actually learns through patterns, colours and spacial awareness, children will probably have to keep on writing out books and books full of information written in straight lines in blue/black ink.

Just think how much content in books written and printed over the past 150 years has just been copied into other books written by students?

How many bytes of computer drive space are full of words just copied from other books and the Internet?

Since you probably don't want to go back to school, I'm going to let you into a few secrets to help you learn in a more effective and efficient way.

Hopefully, our children and future generations will be able to learn in ways that are more natural to the brain that will make their lives easier and more fun.

So this exercise will help to begin to change the way you respond to templates that have been laid down through your formative years.

The exercise will be best undertaken through recording the instructions and playing them back as you relax in a quiet place.

Break Out!

Sit in a comfortable position with both feet on the floor.

Close your eyes and go "inside".

Take a deep breath in and as you breathe out, let go and relax.

In your mind, imagine you are in a long corridor with many doors leading to rooms off.

As you face along the corridor, you begin to experience the feeling of drifting, moving gently backwards, as if floating backwards.

Let go even more and allow the feeling to take you and be aware of the doors along either side of you along the corridor moving past, quicker and quicker.

As you do this, become aware of time moving backwards.

Notice your clothes are becoming dated and you are feeling younger.

As you begin to slow down, recognise that you are in your old school corridor.

As you slow to a stop, be aware now of the surrounding of your school.

See what you see

Hear the sounds of many young voices as they gather around you.

Notice a pencil case in your hand.

See a teacher as they open the door to the exam room and you file in.

Recognise the feeling as you sit at an old wooden desk.

Notice the back of your hand as you hold the pencil case.

Look around the room.

See the teacher handing out the exam papers.

How does that feel?

Notice the feelings in your stomach. .

Do you feel light headed?

Think about this whole situation.

Open your eyes.

Take a deep breath, breath out and relax.

Think of something completely different to reboot your mind.

You're back in the present.

The purpose of that was to get you to remember what it was like to undergo that exam situation.

You can learn the techniques in this book without all that stress.

By relaxing, through visualisation and the proper use of your Reality Simulator, you can experience learning in ways that the brain naturally uses.

Let us consider parenting.

If parents didn't have to go to work, if they could stay at home and spend more time with their kids, then everyone assumes children would be better behaved and better educated.

True or false?

Maybe it's a matter of opinion.

However, put yourself in the position of a young person. Would you really want to be with your parents or carers at home all day?

Do you really think it would make a difference to you?

Surely young people still need to find their own way and have the freedom to experiment, try things out and see what works for them?

I don't suppose for one moment that people set out to be poor parents.

I'm sure everyone gives it their best shot, but it's just that things tend to get in the way.

Through peer pressure, it becomes popular NOT to respect parents and older people. Young people, even if they really do respect or even admire their parents and elders they rarely admit it.

The "generation gap" is a reality when it comes to parents trying to help and influence their children for the best.

So is there any hope for parents or are we all destined for the inevitable breakdown in communications that seems to affect most familial relationships?

In many ways, children pick up learned habits from parents and elders.

The ways they behave at home and outside of the home can be the result of cultural hand-me-downs such as the way you eat, dress, and speak and also the manners you pick up and whether you show respect to others.

If a parental or elder figure is particularly influential or even bigoted in their views, this can seriously impair a young person's personal development in creating their own world-view.

Break Out!

Sit in a comfortable position with both feet on the floor.

Close your eyes and go "inside".

Take a deep breath in and as you breathe out, let go and relax.

In your mind, see a scenario where you are younger, school age, outside, playing with friends.

Notice how much darker the sky has suddenly become and there is a cooler breeze beginning the blow around you now.

Your friends are talking about getting home now. In fact you're aware that you have stayed out far too long.

They begin to gather their things together.

How do you feel about going home?

Would you rather stay out?

If you feel comfortable about going home, if you look forward to going home, then open your eyes and relax.

If you feel wary, if there is a churning in the stomach, then keep your eyes closed and take a deep breath in.

Hold it.

Breathe out.

Gather your belongings and head home.

Push open the door to your house.

How does that feel?

Go inside and hear the voices.

Wash your hands and go in for your meal.

What do you see?

Who is there?

How do they look?

Sit at the table.

Is there a parental figure you are frightened of? Or do you just hold contempt for them?

Gently float out of your body and into the body of that other person.

See through their eyes, hear through their ears and feel their feelings.

As you see yourself "over there", feel the love of the person whose body you now occupy.

Sense their love for you.

The worry and anxiety they have felt because you were late and they didn't know where you were.

How does your reaction to them feel now?

If you've held any sort of grudge against them, can you let that go?

Float back out of their body and into your own body.

Can you, now, tell them how you feel?

Can you tell them you're sorry?

And as they smile and say, "I forgive you", can you forgive yourself for harbouring those feelings for so long?

Take a deep breath and let it go.

Open your eyes and relax.

Think of something completely different to reboot your mind.

How does that feel, now?

You see, in most cases, parents and elders get angry or frustrated because they want to be so good at what they do. They want to help, they want to be friends and in a lot of cases they just feel inadequate.

Many times, children only really appreciate their parents when it's too late.

Young people quite often get along with their parents once they have matured themselves, left home and have got out of the immediate situation.

If you have parents or carers you can forgive and let go, go and do it as soon as you can.

If you can't because they are not around anymore, by using the visualisation techniques you can be free. Remember your brain doesn't know the difference between a real and vividly imagined event.

You could even have someone stand in as a surrogate, if you need a hug.

Please don't hold grudges. Life's not that long and it's really not worth it.

Human beings, unlike animals, have an amazing ability to be self-aware. We can watch ourselves, criticise ourselves, congratulate ourselves, and even argue with ourselves.

We seem to have evolved this ability to enable us to challenge and move on as a species.

We are not content to stand still.

Watch a cat and see how happy it appears to be when it just sits or sleeps. Every "cat day" is the same, but the cat doesn't seem to be too bothered.

You don't see that cat making plans for the future or fretting about how many mice it may need to catch next month to meet targets?

They don't seem too target oriented, do they?

However, humans are always planning, revising, re-planning and working out future scenarios.

As mentioned elsewhere in this book, we have to have goals and meaning in our lives or we will tend to drift out of control.

So it would be good to gain control of this ability and to use it against stress.

Worry is anxiety about the future and in most cases a future created by us in our watching self; it is a self-generated possible future that we are worried about.

We simulate our own possible future and then we worry about how it's going to turn out!

It is much more useful to use the "Reality Simulator" of your mind to create positive future scenarios rather than things to worry about.

It all comes together when you realise that everything in this world that has been created that is not natural is created through thoughts generated in the human mind.

It is literally "our" world system, created by humans, for humans.

So, rather than be a victim, let's make friends with this Watcher in the mind and get it to work for us!

Break Out!

You have already experienced the Watching Self by doing the exercise in Chapter 2. Do this again now.

Sit in a comfortable position with both feet on the floor.

Close your eyes and go "inside".

Take a deep breath in and as you breathe out, let go and relax.

Become aware of watching yourself.

That which is watching cannot be watched.

It is the "Core" of you.

It is the eternal you.

It is beyond any measurement or tangible expression.

As you relax just "Forget" your name.

Lose that label and any other form of identity.

Let go of anything that labels you or links you to external experience or environment.

Once you've got that, you have begun to recognise your Core self.

Rest for moment and enjoy the complete peace of having no identity.

How does your stress level feel now?

In your mind now imagine a time in the near future that you are anticipating as being potentially stressful.

Drift into that situation.

See it, feel it, hear it.

Now change it.

Utilise your Reality Simulator to actually change your potential future.

Change it for the better

Change it to your advantage

Now how does that feel?

Take a deep breath, open your eyes and relax.

Think of something completely different to reboot your mind.

Welcome back.

How does that feel, now?

Do you ever feel that you are a victim of your own thought processes?

This can be a particular source of stress.

As I have pointed out earlier, humans have the unique ability to create a future scenario in their imagination and then turn that into something that may go wrong for them and consequently they worry about it.

When you think about it, how did you learn to do that?

Why on earth would you want to do that?

Think about it again.

You create an imaginary future in which things go wrong.

As a result of this you worry about something that not only might never happen, but you have created out of your own imagination.

It becomes habitual thinking.

Like anything else, the brain generalises in principles.

So you think negative outcomes as a habit.

So can you change that "habit"?

Of course you can.

Just like anything else that goes on in YOUR brain, YOU can change it.

Sometimes, you may just need help from another person.

Therapy can be said to be like jump-starting your car when its starter engine has failed.

Hypnosis techniques are a bit like that, but it gets directly to the point of the problem.

Your conscious mind is a bit like a gatekeeper to your unconscious mind. You could also liken it to a caretaker or a commissionaire.

Your conscious mind is rational, reasoning, questioning everything that it receives by way of date through the senses from the external environment.

Many of the suggestions in the exercises in this book will be resisted by your conscious mind.

It will try to logically interpret them and try to reject them as "silly" or "nonsense".

But it has been proven that the unconscious mind, when accessed through hypnosis or trance, does not provide such resistance.

In fact, when you are in the REM state during your normal sleep time, you probably experience some pretty silly and nonsense dreams do you not?

And it's during those dreams that a lot of learning is undertaken and a lot of emotions are discharged and situations sorted out.

As hypnosis or trance simply re-creates the REM state in order for a therapist or even you yourself to make specific suggestions to improve your life, then why not fully utilise the system?

Hypnosis or trance is like lifting the hood of the car to get directly to the engine to fine-tune it.

It's like taking the back off the TV set to re-tune it.

Someone once said that if you want to take an elephant on a train, the best way is to walk it along the track because that way you will by-pass the ticket office and confuse the stationmaster, both of whom are authority figures metaphorically representing the conscious mind.

You could ask that if the conscious mind is such a good gatekeeper, shouldn't we let it keep the gate, and not try to bypass it?

I would propose that some of the attitudes learned and acted up by the gatekeeper of our unconscious can be a little restricting and not always for a total good for us in a holistic way.

What I mean is that the conscious mind can be fiercely protective of the habits and structures we have built around us over time.

By restricting our experience, it can keep us safe. But it can also fix us into habits that are not for our overall good.

For example, a wariness of the future is good if it is based on and built upon past experiences that may have caused hurt or pain.

However, if that wariness becomes generalised so that you start to fear the future in case there may be hurt out there somewhere, it begins to become an obsession, a phobia, and this will restrict your life and growth as a human being.

By identifying those things that create stress and obsessive behaviour we can begin to change the mind's perception and thus release creativity and spare capacity.

Much less energy will be used in maintaining phobic responses to stimuli and this will free up spare capacity for a bit of fun!

So through hypnosis or trance, you can re-train your unconscious mind to think differently and it will then gradually (or sometimes very quickly) influence your conscious mind.

The unconscious mind is active 24/7 and controls your emotions. If you can begin to get it to relax and anticipate a good future just imagine how much better you are going to feel?

Take the habit of smoking for example.

Many people smoke because they have been led to believe that it helps them relieve stress.

In fact, the chemicals in cigarettes can hijack that part of the brain that produces endorphins; they are the chemicals that make you feel good.

So you are being fooled into thinking it's the cigarettes that make you feel good when in fact you already have that innate capacity to do that just by releasing endorphins through exercise, laughing or experiencing deep pleasure – all of which are activities which are free!

But this is not a book on how to quit smoking, so I rest my case at this point.

Where I am going with this, is to make the point that you have the ability to regain control of your brain and your mind and your body.

Sometimes life on this planet, in this worldly system, is just very negative and you will feel like swimming against a very strong current when you try to be positive for just a short time.

People, media and circumstances seem to try to conspire against your efforts.

However, remember that you create with your mind, and part of that creation is future scenarios.

Break Out!

Sit in a comfortable position with both feet on the floor.

Close your eyes and go "inside".

Take a deep breath in and as you breathe out, let go and relax.

In your imagination travel forwards to a time, in the not too far distant future, to an event you are worried about.

It may be the dentist, a hospital appointment, a meeting with a difficult person, or a test or examination of some kind.

Let your imagination run its natural course and watch the event like you were watching a movie or a TV programme.

Be aware of your feelings all the time.

If you see a good outcome, then fine.

If you see a negative outcome, then run the movie again.

This time, create some additional crisis and notice how you feel about that.

OK, now run it again, but this time you are in control of the movie. You are the director.

Imagine you are sitting in your director's chair with "Spielberg" written on the back.

Watch the movie on your terms.

See the characters doing what you want them to do.

Notice your reactions.

Now how does that feel?

OK, come back out, take a deep breath, let go and open your eyes.

You can do this as often as you like until you create a new habit, lay down a new template in your unconscious mind.

Some might say this is cheating!

Some might say it's manipulating the future!

I say to that, nonsense!

How can you manipulate something that has not happened yet?

That may never happen anyway!

You are changing your own mind.

What's wrong with that?

Some might say that you are creating a happy, positive expectation that may well result in disappointment.

Well, let them say it. If you feel that way, maybe this is the wrong sort of book for you.

All I am suggesting is that by a very small shift in perception, you have changed your outlook on possible future event.

Instead of worrying about a future event, you can now plan for an outcome you want to achieve.

And because all the characters in that scenario are just in your imagination, you can play about with them.

If one of them is a difficult character, make them shorter and give them a pink fluffy tail!

If there is someone who intimidates you, give him or her a Mickey Mouse voice and a flowery hat.

You can do whatever you want because it's your show and you're the director!

Break Out!

Sit in a comfortable position with both feet on the floor.

Close your eyes and go "inside".

Take a deep breath in and as you breathe out, let go and relax.

Travel forward again to that anticipated future event.

Now, this time as the events unfold in a way that you direct them, watch how you react on that screen

See how much calmer and in control you are when faced with the interview panel who are dressed as characters from the Wizard of Oz!

Now gently drift into yourself in that movie.

See what you see and hear what you hear from the inside.

Get close to those characters and enjoy the show.

Have a great time!

It's free!

Ok, think of something completely different to reboot your mind.

Why haven't you done this before?

Probably because no-one's suggested to you that you can.

And you can, you can, you can!

Why not do it again, go somewhere else?

Practice as much as you can until you just can't worry any more.

OK, come back out, take a deep breath, let go and open your eyes.

If you experienced any difficulties with that, get someone to help you with it.

Persevere with it.

I promise it will produce results and reduce your stress in anticipating the future.

There's just one more thing I'd like to suggest to help you manage your thoughts.

These thoughts just keep coming, don't they? Your mind is like a ticker tape machine sending out streams of thoughts all the time.

Where do they come from?

Why are they running through all the time?

It would be good to notice how they run and if there is any pattern here.

Break Out!

Sit in a comfortable position with both feet on the floor.

Close your eyes and go "inside".

Take a deep breath in and as you breathe out, let go and relax.

Turn your attention completely to your thoughts.

Rest for about two minutes and just let the thoughts settle into a pattern.

Notice if you have a train of thoughts, jumping from one thing to another or if it is many thoughts but they all link to one subject or theme.

If you recognise a theme, create in your imagination a big white filing cabinet and label one drawer according to that theme.

Take your thoughts and put them in that drawer, close it.

If you recognise that there are still further thoughts on another theme, label another draw and put them inside, close the drawer.

When you've done that with all the available thoughts, lock the cabinet.

If you have any residual, random thoughts just let them drift away.

Now rest for a few moments and try to keep a blank mind.

Unlock and cabinet and open one of the drawers, taking out the thoughts in that drawer.

Can you recapture them?

Are they as strong or intense?

OK, come back out, take a deep breath, let go and open your eyes.

Whatever your experience, you have begun to take control of your thoughts.

This is an excellent exercise to train your mind.

Break Out!

Sit in a comfortable position with both feet on the floor.

Close your eyes and go "inside".

Take a deep breath in and as you breathe out, let go and relax.

Imagine yourself walking along a path, perhaps by some woods or in a park.

Notice the cool air of early Fall and the wonderful shades of colour of the leaves on the trees.

Reds, oranges and browns.

Blowing softly in the breeze.

Some leaves drifting slowly from the trees in the air around you before settling on the path and the grass alongside.

The path leads you down to a free flowing stream nestled beneath some larger trees that overhang the water.

Sit yourself down on the grassy bank beside the river.

Watch the water flowing past.

It comes along from upstream, flowing freely and regularly.

It's a constant stream of free flowing water.

Notice the leaves that have fallen into the water being carried along from upstream.

Watch them as they drift past and continue downstream.

Those leaves are like your thoughts.

They come from somewhere upstream but you can't see the source.

They float past.

They continue downstream but you can't see where they end up.

You can't see the result of their journey.

If you were to reach down and pick one out of the water, what would happen?

Would the flow stop?

Would it change anything?

If you stop one of your thoughts and pick it up and act upon it, would it make any difference?

Or could you just keep letting them drift past?

Would it really make any difference?

OK, come back out, take a deep breath, let go and open your eyes.

If you tend to act on all or most of your thoughts, try just letting them float by for a day or so and see what happens.

You might be pleasantly surprised that you don't need to act on them all the time. That you could actually choose which ones you want to act on.

You can select.

It's your thoughts.

It's your brain.

It's your mind, and it's a wonderful piece of kit, if used properly.

One more exercise to help you relax and you can really have a bit of fun with this:

Break Out!

Maybe you have thoughts that convert to images in your mind that trouble you.

For example, I knew someone who, after a busy day, would be subjected with images of crowds of people all seemingly asking her to do things or accusing her of not doing things she should have done.

I suggested that she concentrate on that image and see if it is a still or a movie. It turned out that she saw it as if it were on a TV screen.

I got her to turn the image to black and white, shrink it to half size and literally imagine turning off the sound on the TV.

Then I got her to shrink it down half size again.

I then encouraged her to visualise a really pleasant memory or a place I know she loved to visit where there were crowds of people having fun and not asking anything of her.

I then asked her to make that image into a movie, colour it up bright and cheerful and add sounds and smells.

I then asked her to make that moving image twice as big.

Then, turning her attention back to the old black and white shrunken image to now just switch it off and watch the screen turn to blank and be replaced instantly with the pleasant image and turn it up brighter and brighter.

Within minutes she was happy and relaxed and all the negative thoughts had gone.

Give it a go!

Creative Thinking

Everything created in our world system starts with a thought.

Look around you now.

What do you see?

A computer screen and keyboard?

Maybe a laptop or a smart phone?

Maybe a print out of the pages upon which are printed the words you are reading.

The computer screen started with a thought.

A certain Mr Babbage thought about a machine that has now evolved to become the computer you can see.

The keyboard began with a thought of someone who wanted an easier way to input data into the computer.

The mouse is the result of a further thought.

The words you read originated as my thoughts and they are printed with a printer that started as a thought, on paper that started as a thought.

I challenge you to go back along the timeline of anything created in this world that you can think of and not realise that it began with a thought, in someone's mind.

What have you created today?

You don't have to be an inventor to create things.

The building you are in started as a thought in the mind of an architect or designer. They are not categorised as "inventors" but they do invent, don't they?

The majority of the items that form part of our everyday reality are created in the minds of human beings.

It probably seems obvious when you think about it.

But few people are taught to think this way.

How many children are taught at school or by parents that they can create a new reality with their minds?

You can begin to take control of your stress by realising that you are a creator of your reality.

However bad you feel, however low you are, your next thought will create a new reality.

Think about this.

As I've stated elsewhere, your mind does not know the difference between a real and vividly imagined event. This is proven by the fact that creators think ideas into reality. It's the same process that thinks it and then sees it when it's finished.

For example, I have a very good friend who is an architect. He designs buildings, homes, offices and such like. He imagines what it would look like, how it would be constructed and even considers in great detail what it would be like to live or work there.

To him, the idea is so real that he can visualise it and he has computer software which can take his idea as it flows from his mind through his arm into a keyboard or computer mouse and make it look almost real on the screen or paper.

More than that, he can then drop that image into a scene that already exists where the building will eventually be built.

This way he can present a finished scenario to a planning authority in order to obtain permission to build.

Then other people become involved in his creative process.

The Planning Authority will approve the scheme to be built.

A quantity surveyor will provide an estimate of cost. Quantity surveyors are perhaps some of the most "grounded" people on this earth. They literally count the numbers of bricks, nails, screws, roof tiles it will take to build what the architect has imagined.

The quantity surveyor estimates the amount of mortar required to stick the bricks together and how much of every component that goes to make up a new home or office building will be needed.

It is sometimes said within the construction industry that quantity surveyors lack imagination. That it is the architect who has the imagination and the quantity surveyor brings an element of reality to the whole enterprise by counting the cost.

But the quantity surveyor must have wonderful imagination and plays their part fully in playing along with the whole game of reality generation.

The quantity surveyor counts bricks that don't yet exist and measures lengths of piping that doesn't exist for a house or office building that doesn't exist.

Then he comes up with a complete package price for something that doesn't exist yet!

Then a builder will come along and take all that has been imagined so far and create it out of materials that were created through someone else's imagination.

And someone out there in the big wide world has been imagining living in a house or relocating his company into just the sort of place that is being created by that other group of creators.

One day, a little way in the future, the two factors will meet.

The creative processes which builds the house or office and the creative process that inspires somebody to seek out that new house of office will come together as the two meet and deals are struck and moving arrangements are undertaken.

Are you beginning to believe that you do not have to be a victim to circumstances?

Why don't you start to create your own circumstances?

Why don't you start to create your own piece of reality?

But maybe you think that the things that cause your stress are not in your control.

But they are!

Oh, yes they are!

They are, because they are in your realm of influence.

How far do you think your incredibly creative mind can stretch?

Break Out!

Write a list of all the things you have created in your life that began as a thought.

You will be amazed.

Give yourself plenty of time – it could be a long list.

Allow your unconscious mind to bring things back, see what bubbles up.

Enjoy this and give yourself a great big metaphorical pat on the back for being so creative.

Now select one thing from the list and take a virtual journey into the past for a while.

Select one thing that you have created with a thought and which has become a reality in your life.

Maybe it's the home you now live in.

You thought one day, "I think I'll move here, or there", or whatever you thought and that started reality moving along a particular track or in a particular orbit and now here you are.

OK, so now imagine you had a thought that culminated in the first mobile telephone.

Close your eyes and go inside and really use that Reality Simulator to create a daydream where you are the creator of the mobile phone.

Where do you live?

What do you do for enjoyment?

Do you still own and run a business or did you retire early?

Have some fun with it.

Now come back and think, "Why couldn't it have been me?"

Why not?

OK, the mobile phone's already done, but what about all those other things you listed out.

I would like to take a guess that you've thought about something that someone else has made into reality.

So why not take a chance next time?

To ensure that our minds are functioning to their full creative capacity, there is a necessity to undertake a full self-diagnostic and stress audit on a regular basis.

Consider again the computer.

The computer is a wonderful, amazing piece of machinery.

It arrives bright and shiny, starting up swiftly and opening up a world of possibilities for the operator.

There it sits, almost humming gently, anticipating your fingers making that first keystroke or mouse click.

It will continue to do so, until the operator makes the next move.

The operator provides and computer with motivation and direction.

However, after a time, once many programs have been run and there are a few miles on the clock (please excuse the apparent mixed metaphor), it may begin to run a little slower.

The information processed by the computer which serves the operator's needs, will actually slow down the operating speed of the computer.

Like a car, simply by being used, it will begin to tire and slow down as it carries more and more unnecessary baggage.

It is recommended that to keep the computer running at its optimum, regular servicing should take place.

This servicing involves cleaning out old files and programmes, re-organising or de-fragmenting the main hard drive and tuning up performance. There is even the need to regularly clean out little rogue programmes planted there by other people, such as virus programmes or spy ware.

If this is not done, the computer will eventually experience a breakdown, leaving the operator stranded.

So what about our human machine?

Your diagnostics are normally undertaken at night, while you sleep, by your brain.

As long as you sleep for a reasonable period of uninterrupted time to enable the various modes to operate, the dreams to be created and the new learning to be laid down as templates in the REM state, then you will wake every morning having had a "disk defragmentation" and a "virus scan".

Because what's a computer if it isn't a creation of the mind?

And if it's created by the mind, it will reflect the workings of the mind.

However, some hard-wired templates will not be re-programmed overnight, however long we sleep.

Much of the negative conditioning we've received from school, friends and family will be so deeply embedded that it will be difficult to shift.

They can be as stubborn as computer virus programmes.

Do you have a virus, a "Trojan horse" in your mind? Has someone installed a programme that's time releasing negative beliefs?

However, it is possible to start to re-programme and shift those stubborn negative post-hypnotic suggestions from the past that have shaped your consciousness, our personalities and set down patterns of behaviours we seem to be stuck with.

Break Out!

Think of something someone has said to you in the past that has become a belief for you.

It may be one of those, "You'll never be any good at..." moments.

Concentrate on that for a moment.

Is it a voice?

Does it have a face, an identity?

Is it an authoritative voice, such as a teacher or parent or carer?

Where is it? Is it inside or outside of your head?

Once you've located it, turn the volume down by half and make the voice different.

Use a cartoon mouse or duck voice.

If it has a face, give it a big red nose and shaggy hair.

Make it very small.

Stick out your thumb.

Send the silly voice to the end of your thumb.

Does it still sound like it's something you should be taking seriously?

Just flick it off your thumb.

How does that feel?

Come back now and think how good that is!

You need never, ever, be intimidated by voices from your imagination.

The past has gone, the future hasn't arrived, and only the present is now.

Finally, I'd just like to mention the effect that voices and images from the negative world view can have on us all.

I'm referring here not just to people, who may be naturally negative, but mainly the media, written and broadcast TV and their tendency to promote worst-case scenario scaremongering.

For example, have you noticed how natural disasters or accidents are rated according to how many people died? And if no-one dies, they tend to estimate how many people might have died, had the event happened a few hours earlier or a few miles away where there was a crowded stadium or shopping mall.

Just as you can use the "off" switch in the imagined scenarios created by your Reality Simulator, so can you use the "off "switch on your real life TV or radio?

And please, don't watch TV news last thing at night!

Why do they put the most awful news on just before we go to bed?

Little wonder our dreams can be weird sometimes. We are playing out our own parochial emotional situations sometimes on a worldwide stage, mixing our own lives in with those of millions around the world as we sleep.

Is there a worse way to go to bed than following the late night news?

Also, why do we read the papers first thing in the morning! What worse way to start your day than reading the paper at breakfast or commuting to work?

Create your own entertainment.

Break Out!

Do you ever get a glimpse of a memory?

Just maybe a flash of an event from the past?

Let your unconscious mind bubble up a good memory now.

This time, hold it, go with it, and fully return to it.

Don't miss out on the fleeting opportunity your unconscious mind has given you of replaying a great time.

Go on a trip, use the ticket and take a ride in the Reality Simulator.

Add some music.

Make it like a movie.

Then float into it and make it real.

See what you see, hear what you hear and fully enter into that situation.

When you're ready come back.

Think of something completely different and reboot your mind.

Take Control Of Your Body

The food we use to fuel our body will directly affect its performance.

Generally in the West we are becoming less active.

Exercise keeps the metabolic rate up and burns more calories.

20 minutes of aerobic exercise will keep the metabolism at a higher rate for 24 hours after the exercise.

Much of the convenience foods we eat contain highly processed foods and chemicals. It might taste good, but it's created that way. We are fooled by the taste and colour and speed and convenience.

There are hidden contents in some foods.

There is a general lack of knowledge and education about processed foods.

Processed foods containing sugar and refined carbohydrates can de-stabilise blood sugars which does not help to maintain a level blood sugar during the day leading to dips in energy and concentration.

Toxic bodies in the blood can cause cravings.

Through poor diet, some drugs, alcohol, illness and environmental factors toxicity can dwell in the body.

Anxiety can create negative thinking style or "black and white" extreme thinking that causes high cortisol levels and insulin problems.

Diets really rarely work in the long term.

Diets based on will power alone seldom last long.

The conscious mind has a limited capacity to maintain strategies and other priorities can crowd in, overpowering the desire to maintain a diet consciously.

It is much better to leave food control to the unconscious mind that will naturally remind us when it's time to eat by making us hungry!

Cravings however can be caused by physical imbalances resulting from the diet itself as the body tries to maintain a store of fat as it is being deprived of food by our very own attempts to lose weight. We can find that by dieting we are fighting against our own body!

Every mealtime becomes a battlefield as the dieter struggles against psychologically or physically driven cravings.

The brain may have learned a pattern of anticipating food at specific times, perhaps in the evenings after a busy day. The body's stress levels from the day build up the anticipation of food to satisfy cravings. If we deny it that food, it will demand even more!

The pattern learned by the brain, the new template laid down has to be changed if the body is to be brought in line.

We need to provide choices that will encourage healthy eating behaviour patterns.

But we keep trying and every new diet, every different diet; will be the one that works – this time.

However, yo-yo dieting causes the body to store fat.

We need to work with psychological instincts and physical imbalances that promote obsessive thinking about food and overeating.

We need to get a new perspective.

If you've over eaten or found yourself eating without tasting the food, you may have experienced an addictive trance.

This is nothing to worry about because at least now you know about it and therefore you are less likely to do it again. If you do, you will realise it.

Over eating can result from boredom, anxiety or in compensation for feelings of guilt, worthlessness and criticism.

Do you think about food a lot?

Do you eat at specific times?

Do you eat when upset?

Do you eat after a stressful day?

Do you justify eating, telling yourself you deserve it?

Do other people influence you to eat or drink?

Do you ever feel full or hungry?

Do you get anxious around food?

If you find that you identify a pattern involving food, then you can start to break its habitual hold over you.

Identify the pattern that's causing your poor eating or drinking habits.

Maybe you eat food or drink alcohol late at night?

There may be a trigger that starts you off.

It could be that you just believe that you deserve a drink because you've had such a busy day?

Where did that idea come from?

Surely you deserve not to drink? Surely you deserve to enjoy a full evening, not get knocked out halfway through by eating rubbish food and drinking?

There's an exercise called scrambling which follows later in this module that can help to break up unhealthy eating patterns.

Set realistic goals for weight loss – don't create more stress!

Relaxation is so important.

Think of your body like the most perfect motorcar, but even this will perform poorly if the wrong grade of petrol is used.

Slow down your eating.

Enjoy food consciously.

A stable and balanced diet can be maintained if the essentials of good diet are adhered to, blood sugars stabilised, basic emotional needs met, relaxation, optimistic outlook.

So give the diet a miss and adopt a new way of eating for life

Throw away the scales – measure another way

Be aware of sugar dips and drinking water before meal (not too much) dilutes digestive enzymes.

Important things to remember:

- Eat only when hungry
- Sit at a table
- Eat consciously
- Have fun

Some say you are what you eat.

That can sound like a cliché but it is very true.

Basic nutrition is vital to maintaining a healthy, balanced body function. It is important to have a body which is able to respond readily to the demands of life, ready to go into action when the brain demands and able to react correctly when under different types of pressure.

Just as a car needs a regular service to keep it running efficiently, or a computer needs its hard drive de-fragmented, so your body and mind need to be regularly serviced or cleaned up.

If you have owned a car or a motorcycle and not regularly checked and cleaned the body it will begin to become dull, lose its sheen and its ability to reflect its surroundings, showing its true colours in the best light to those who observe it.

The vehicle almost seems to lose its self-esteem, no longer the proud beast it once was when new.

If the inside of the car is not regularly cleaned, it also becomes tired and jaded. The interior fabric fades and loses its lustre. The windows now longer clean, so it is more difficult to make out the road ahead and be sure of the clarity of your direction.

Then there's the engine itself. If not regularly cleaned and serviced it will become sluggish, misfire, use more fuel but perform less efficiently. It will almost seem an effort for it to pull the body along the road.

If it becomes clogged with carbon residues and it will begin the smell and resist your efforts to drive it to its best ability.

However, the engine is actually not what makes the car go. The engine only responds to the instructions provided by the driver through the interface between mechanical and biological.

Amazingly, the car is equipped with gadgets that enable the human to communicate with it and issue instructions.

A key, some pedals, gearshift, brakes, knobs and switches.

Without these the car would never move.

The driver is the "life" in the body of the car.

The driver provides the car with motivation and direction.

The car responds, the team works together to make the journey to the destination.

But if the car is not regularly serviced it will eventually experience a breakdown, perhaps leaving the driver stranded.

We have the innate resources to get our nutritional requirements met and the basic desires of hunger and fullness should drive our actions when it comes to food and drink.

However, our inbuilt mechanisms are surprisingly easily derailed.

There is wide public ignorance about health and nutrition.

There is much contradictory information in the media. This week coffee is bad for us, and then next week it's not. One week red wine is bad for us, and then it's not. And so on.

We are also constantly being bombarded with promotions and advertising for unhealthy "ideals".

Much of the time, the emphasis in the media is about weight, to the detriment of overall balanced health.

The food we eat influences our

- Mood
- Appearance
- Concentration
- Self-perception
- Cognitive function
- Energy levels

It is useful to consider nutrition in food groups.

Each food group has a particular function in the body.

The glycaemic index is used to measure the rate at which food is converted into energy.

- Carbohydrates – simple or complex
- Proteins
- Fats – essential or non-essential

A balanced nutritional plan will be required to cement and maintain the work you undertake based on the exercises in this book.

Your diet will assist in improving your concentration, energy and mood.

Here are some basic facts about nutrition. It will be extremely important for you to obtain quality information relating to your own personal situation via your own health practitioner or clinic.

All food groups are transformed into glucose or glycogen.

The brain takes about 30% of energy produced in the body.

To maximise and stabilise energy levels and improve overall function you need to:

• Eat a balance of the food groups

• Minimise the foods that steal your energy such as coffee, highly processed man made refined foods and sugar.

It is vital to maintain blood sugar levels throughout the day.

This will avoid a rollercoaster of hyper highs and tired lows throughout the day.

It's best to "graze" a little and often through the day.

Going without food for too long, or eating too many quickly converting foods, leads to poor concentration, tiredness and cravings for more of the wrong foods.

Intake of the wrong type of food will lead to your body craving for more of the same stuff!

Chemical toxicity from manufactured foods causes damage to the body.

Certain ingredients are added to such foods in manufacture to create and add fluids to bypass natural responses and influence people to eat more. It's a money business.

Processed food releases opiates via trans-fats, by passing the feeling of being full so that you will eat more.

Sugar is easily converted into blood glucose, which triggers the release of insulin to prevent the levels of glucose from becoming high.

The extra glucose is stored in the pancreas and as fat in the body.

That body fat collects precisely in the places you really don't want it. In females it will probably be round the middle and thighs. In men, it will be around the middle and the chest. Do you really want saddlebags or man boobs?

The body shape may be a reliable indicator as to high levels of sugar storage which can result from yo-yo dieting where the body stores what you do eat as it anticipates a time of starvation ahead.

It's simply another pattern that it quickly picks up and adjusts to compensate for.

However hard you try, you cannot fool your body, nor can you, for very long, persuade it to operate in a way that it simply wasn't designed to.

In terms of over eating, this is often actually the result of poor diet because the body is not working effectively and we feel that we have to stoke up with quick food to keep us going. This, in turn, can lead to cravings.

The food we eat has a profound effect on an hourly, daily and accumulative basis.

This affects our emotional and physical wellbeing.

At the end of the day, this is all about the basic needs of human beings to operate in accordance with the "manufacturer's instructions" for our body and the mind which keeps it functioning.

Sometimes our basic needs are met in inappropriate ways.

Our search for a basic need (such as security or love) that may be missing can result in eating habits to satisfy that need.

Those innate templates are off-track.

If you can stick to the basic principle that when your body requires fuel you will feel hunger in that body and an innate desire to go and hunt for food you can't go far wrong.

However, when you go hunting, make sure you "hunt" the right stuff at the supermarket!

Remember that stress puts the body on alert, creates that flight or fight response and set up craving for carbohydrate kicks to fuel up for a potential period of high energy activity with little intake of food for perhaps a sustained period of time.

Take the basic situation when we were functioning in the wilds of the young planet Earth and we were literally hunters in the wild.

We are hungry, basic instincts driving us to find food.

We are confronted by a sabre tooth tiger so the body goes into flight or fight response.

Will it eat me, or will I eat it?

That's ok for a short while.

Bring the situation up to date.

You are in your modern day hunting ground – the office or sales pitch.

You have been on demand for about six hours and suddenly some "prey" comes into sight. You have to react, quickly and you have to be at your best.

The "prey" turns out to be the boss demanding a report by the end of the day.

The same old stress reaction kicks in.

You are human, after all.

Your body needs fuel to cope with the heightened stress levels and creates a craving sensation.

You need to hunt, quickly.

Do you hunt out tuna or nuts?

No, you hunt out the brightly coloured Coke machine and a packet of crisps, perhaps some chocolate.

You experience a high, which lasts about an hour. Sufficient to complete the report but afterwards your sugar level will plummet and you will desperately crave more.

What better way than a beer or glass of wine at the end of the day, on the way home.

Then perhaps you have another one or two when you get home.

You may end up eating a microwave meal later or hunting down a takeaway.

That night, your body is trying to bring a balance to your blood sugar and process the intake that will probably make for a difficult night's rest.

Your brain will be processing the day's events and those unresolved emotional reactions you had to your boss's demands to get the report finished.

That will add to a difficult night.

You awake next morning to a new day but it will probably just feel like a continuation of the previous day and the cycle begins all over again.

You can break this cycle through a sustained intake of quality food and drink throughout the day.

You will find that you will be ready and prepared for any sudden response required to deal with unexpected situations.

Break Out!

So, try the next exercise that involves a technique called "scrambling".

The point of this is to break up a pattern of thinking that creates a problem for you and then replace it with a better, healthier pattern.

For example, you may habitually eat junk food after 8 o'clock in the evening and that will result in you probably not sleeping as well as you could because your body will be struggling to digest and your rest may not be as deep as you need it to be.

So scrambling will change the pattern and set you free to make other choices.

It's certainly best to work with a friend or partner who can help you break up the pattern but also ensure you are not "self-deceiving" when it comes to identifying the "trigger" that starts the habitual pattern.

That habitual pattern may start with a trigger such as a thought like, "I've had a bad day, so now I deserve a glass of wine and an ice cream" or "When my friend comes round we always have a bottle of wine together".

The trigger may also be an event, such as a TV programme or that hungry feeling you may get at 8pm.

So for example, I had a problem with nail biting. I worked with a partner to identify the trigger that started me nail biting and then about eight different events which occurred regularly around my nail biting, such as the fingers going to the mouth, the chewing, the spitting etc. – not very nice, I know!

This exercise is quite complex and really needs a friend or partner to work with but it's well worthwhile.

So, let's give it a go.

On a piece of paper, write down a pattern you would like to change. Think about HOW you do the pattern of behaviour you want to change.

Write down the trigger. Also make a note of what emotions and feelings are attached to the activity around the trigger, such as feeling bored.

Then write down up to 4 other activities that follow the trigger and make up the UNWANTED behaviour.

Write them in the order they happen, with the trigger activity first.

For example, it may be that the TV programme starts, then you go to the kitchen, then you get food out of the fridge, then you prepare it, then you eat it, then you regret it.

When you have a number of points, ask your partner to read them, and fully understand each event.

Now think of a sequence of events you would prefer to happen following the trigger. For example, when you get bored, go for a walk or read a book or make a healthy snack.

Now write down the trigger and the steps for the DESIRED behaviour pattern.

Now, you relax and close your eyes.

Your partner reads through the UNWANTED pattern once as you imagine going through the sequence.

See what you see, hear what you hear and fully return to the event.

Now go through it again, in more concentrated detail.

It's important that after each step, you open your eyes to evoke the "re-boot" effect and close them again to enable yourself to fully enter into the next step.

By doing this you are literally confusing that part of the brain that creates memories and imagines future events and it won't know the difference between the two!

Repeat this for every step of the UNWANTED behaviour pattern.

OK, then your partner will run through the steps again with you in the same way (eyes closed, open, closed etc.) BUT IN A COMPLETELY RANDOM ORDER.

For example, you start with preparing the food, then you're regretting eating it, then the TV programme starts, then you're going to the fridge, then you're going to the kitchen, now the TV programme starts, now you're regretting it, and so on and so on.

The important thing is that your partner reads the scrambled schedule of events to you, and it may take three of four runs through in a completely different sequence each time.

You start relaxed with your eyes closed and as your partner reads the event, you fully return to it and experience it. Then, before the next event is read out, you open your eyes and close them again.

So it goes:

Close eyes, partner reads first step and you imagine it, open eyes.

Close eyes, partner reads next step and you imagine it, open eyes.

And so on through the scrambled pattern.

Once that's done, ask your partner to read you through the DESIRED behaviour as you fully enter into the activity in your imagination.

Afterwards see how you feel about that pattern and you'll be amazed at how you can "re-programme" your thinking in this way, which will change your behaviour.

Scrambling can also be done slightly differently and simpler way if you are unable to find a partner.

On a piece of paper, write down a pattern you would like to change. Think about HOW you do the pattern of behaviour you want to change.

Write down the trigger. Also make a note of what emotions and feelings are attached to the activity around the trigger, such as feeling bored.

Then write down what happens at the end of the pattern or sequence of events and think about how you feel afterwards.

For example, it may be that the TV programme starts and that's the trigger, then you go to the kitchen, then you get food out of the fridge, then you prepare it, then you eat it, then you regret it, and that feeling of regret is the end of the pattern.

So imagine you're just about to do the action arising from the trigger. Really enter into it, see what you see and hear what you hear and really sense the feelings involved.

But just as you're about to do the next thing in the sequence, jump right to the end event. Jump right to that feeling of regret.

Do this up to five times until you know the pattern has been interrupted and your mind has associated the feeling of regret with the trigger and thus the compulsion to do the behaviour is broken.

Afterwards see how you feel about that pattern and you'll be amazed at how you can "re-programme" your thinking in this way, which will change your behaviour.

Good.

Remember when visualising a future state, create a "multi-sensory" focused future image, create hope for your future – it's your show!

In order to lay down new templates, you can start with small changes,

A flower turns to the light, however small or weak the sunray.

Sometimes you can simply enjoy walking or stretching but whatever you do, do more active stuff.

It really doesn't have to be drastic, just get going.

Walk to shops, post letters in a post box a few streets away.

Here is a Top Ten of ideal dietary and nutritional staples: (in no particular order, because they are all equally important)

Create time to eat

Take time out to really appreciate and enjoy meal times.

Fuel your body regularly

"Grazing" little and often will help avoid energy and concentration dips.

Eat Breakfast

Essential, sets up the metabolism for the day and basic to controlling weight long term.

Eat a variety of foods

Try not to get stuck in shopping ruts; be adventurous with your meal planning

Eat protein with complex carbohydrates

Maintains a steady flow of energy, as the body will convert these foods into glucose more slowly and minimise fat storage

Stay hydrated

Drink plenty of water – up to 1.5 litres per day. If your body tells you that you are thirsty, you are probably already dehydrated. Limit alcohol and salt intake.

Avoid sugar

The speed at which sugar converts to blood glucose creates a quick high followed by a resultant low causing hunger pangs.

Eat the right type of fat

Omega 3 and omega 6 are essentials but go for less saturated fat.

Exercise

Aim to fit in about 30 minutes of exercise about 3 times a week.

Follow the 80% rule

You can blow it, every once in a while. 80 percent
of the times you need to stick to healthy eating
and exercising. Remember, don't diet!

Self-Image

Self-image is not so much about your body that
will find its naturally healthy and proper state
through diet and exercise, but rather that which
you project to other people and which may
actually be a cover for the real you.

Self-image can be how you perceive yourself and
that which you project out to other people and
maintaining that projection takes up a lot of your
own resources in terms of energy.

Projecting and maintaining a self-image can be
exhausting, utilising much of the energy you
need to maintain a balanced life.

Projecting an image can also lead to a distorted
view of your physical self, leading to eating
disorders or body dysmorphia which is where
people actually don't believe the image they see
in a mirror and perceive themselves to be uglier
or fatter than they really are.

If you can make sure that you are not
maintaining a projected image, you can be really
honest with yourself and others as you gain
control over your mind and body.

How you think of yourself will be a vital element in the stress to success journey.

Self-image is the way you see yourself in your imagination.

We tend to overlay our core, real self with that which we sometimes refer to as our "personality" which can be created from "drivers" which we inherit from our history, culture, education, family and so on.

We often need to maintain these drivers to be considered "viable" and "relevant" in our society and in order to get a job and so on.

This "personality" is not the real core self but carries the baggage of life and stressors can hook onto it.

To appear "in control" we may even overlay this with another positive projected self-image.

This third part is the part that conceals those "weaknesses" such as addictions, phobias, compulsions, attitudes and poor behavioural patterns.

We project the "overlay" of the third image to others because we don't want others to detect any weakness.

Hypnosis breaks through this projected image to deal with the issues connected to the second part and gradually the core self, the real self, is able to break through.

This may all sound a bit schizophrenic, but it's not like that.

This is nothing to worry about.

It's an awareness of where stress may have got its hooks into you and such awareness will begin to bring release.

How about trying out an exercise that will begin to break down those parts that are not the real, core you?

If it is active, this will involve turning off that image projector for a while.

Then we can begin to unhook the baggage from the personality.

Finally, your core, real self will begin to shine through.

Break Out!

Consider your self image, how you "see" yourself.

Think about that now.

How do you see yourself?

What age are you?

How tall are you?

What weight are you?

Do you always feel the same age or have you felt the same age for some time?

If you didn't know your age, what age would you think you are?

Spend some time with this.

Now recall the earlier exercise when you forgot your name and now unhooked yourself from any labels, your job, your family, your home and all the things which you carry around which identify you as you in the world system.

Connect to the core you.

How different is that from your self-image?

Now think about the image you project to others.

Is that based on the real, core you?

Is it based on your self-image?

Or is it a third option? Is it almost like a suit of armour, or a projection to please other's expectations?

OK, take a deep breath, open your eyes and come back out.

Think of something different to re-boot your mind.

If you are happy that your core self is dominant then by practising the exercises which utilise the "Watching Self" you will strengthen that core and understand that you can separate your core self from any stress which has hooked itself onto your overlaid personality.

This will be a matter of time and practising new behaviour patterns.

If you find that your overlaid "personality" is dominating your core self, then you may be quite prone to influence by others and the world system which carries the "stress virus" which has hooked onto that part of you.

If you find that you are also projecting that third image, this will gradually fade as your core self-gains dominance.

The main thing is that you become aware of those parts of you and as you gain control, these will morph into the perfect you.

Break Out!

Sit with your feet on the floor, close your eyes and relax.

Just concentrate on your breathing and go "inside".

Now practise disconnecting with your name and any other form of identity with the world system.

Shake loose your connections with family, friends and your career or job.

Shake loose from your home, your community and the town or city in which you live.

In your imagination, create a field of lush green grass under a clear blue sky.

Now imagine another "you" standing in front of you.

This is an amazing you, a perfect you, an uncontaminated you.

Look at the way that other you is standing and their posture, confidence and control.

Drift into that other, perfect you.

Notice how it feels.

Drift back out.

Now imagine a situation in the future that you have been anticipating.

It may be a party, an event, a celebration.

Make it some event where you will be with friends and family.

Watch that event on a TV screen in your mind.

Watch the other, ideal, perfect you in that situation.

Watch how that you interacts with people.

How you walk and talk and hold the room with your ease and control.

Now drift into that screen.

Step into that ideal you.

See through your eyes, hear through your ears and fully engage in the event.

Notice the reaction of your friends and family.

Be aware of how confident and in control you feel.

You see, it is possible to be your true, core, real, perfect self.

Take some time to consider two or three other situations where you watch your core self "in the flesh" interacting with work, family and friends and then drift in and fully engage with the experience.

When you're done, take a deep breath and open your eyes, come back out.

Think of something completely different to reboot your mind.

Practice this exercise to strengthen your core self.

Remember, your core self, even when in the flesh, has nothing for stress to hook onto.

There is more on how our personalities can be made up from "parts" in the next module.

Reframing & Re-focusing

The way you think really determines the way you perceive the external environment (which you might refer to as the world) and the inner reality in which we all make re-presentations of that external environment.

Shakespeare is credited with the saying:

"There is nothing either good or bad but thinking makes it so."

The way you explain things to yourself, the way you interpret things, gives meaning to events and creates your reality.

You tend to attach meaning to all of your experiences, shaping your world and your views of people.

Sometimes people get stuck, seeing a problem from only one perspective. We sometimes need an externally applied re-boot to free up our minds when they have got stuck with a learned pattern that has created an unrealistic or unhealthy perspective on life.

We can even self-deceive as we warp events to suit our perspective.

This sometimes happens to the degree that we enter into a "Pity Party" of self-delusion and even when someone offers a lifeline we either refuse to see it or refuse to accept it.

Reframing happens in everyday life and can be very effective in changing your or someone else's viewpoint.

It allows us to see a situation from another viewpoint but can also significantly shift the meaning of a situation and can even make it impossible for someone to see the situation as a problem anymore.

One problem is that it can seem like too easy an answer or way out if you feel really stressed out.

You will be able to understand the benefits of reframing.

Even offering multiple perspectives can help to break fixed views and this is where changing perception and visualisation can help.

It is good to get a new window on reality when you encounter a situation that gives you uneasy feelings.

You can use the Watching Self to see things from another view or even another person's perspective.

You can virtual time travel to a point after the event or you can rehearse the event going really well.

Break Out!

Come up with reframes for each of the following "glass half-empty" statements:

"I'm always getting it wrong, I'm such a failure"

"I've tried giving up smoking but always start again."

"Since I sold my car I have to walk everywhere"

"I've only got two real friends and they live miles away"

"I always get into trouble by falling for unreliable people."

Try to come up with some of your own where you can get into a habit of converting half-empty phrases into half-full ones.

Reframing in a way is the start of really beginning to relax about how the world is treating you. Because there are at least two sides to every story and you are becoming an expert in seeing things from many perspectives.

In fact, you have the understanding and awareness that can really begin to make profound changes in the way you behave in order to get to a position where stress will not have anything to hook on to.

It's like the material known as "Velcro".

Velcro has two parts.

The first part could be called the submissive part. This has a surface that consists of a mass of fibres, rather like a very rough fur but made of a nylon or plastic.

On its own, this part doesn't serve any obvious purpose. It is stuck, furry side up, to one surface to which another surface is to be attached.

The second part of the "Velcro" product consists of a mass of tiny nylon or plastic hooks.

Again, on its own, this does not seem to serve any obvious purpose and is pretty benign in terms of a threat.

However, there's a kind of magic to "Velcro" which made the person who had the original thought (remember that!) a huge amount of money.

When the two surfaces are brought together, they stick.

One surface is a receptor. It receives the other.

The other, the hooked surface, attaches itself to the receptor.

They can be separated, but it takes some effort.

One of the miracles of "Velcro" is that it needs no glue or sticky substance to keep the surfaces joined.

They do it themselves.

That is what they are designed to do.

Similarly, stress as the hooked surface, will attach itself to your receptive surface.

Once attached, "Velcro" needs a third party force to pull the two surfaces apart.

Once stress has its hooks into a person, it also quite often takes a third party to pull it away from the receptive person.

The good news is that by utilising your Watching Self, you have that third party to beat that stress which has its hooks into you.

Through a change of perception, through reframing, you can work from the watcher perspective and unhook stress from your receptive surface.

Because your Watching Self does not have the receptive surface.

To use another brilliant mind-created product as an analogy, your Watching Self has a "Teflon" finish. Teflon is used on frying pans.

It has a non-stick surface.

So one of the joys of seeing life from the Watching perspective is that you can see your receptive self with the stress attached and you can peel away that stress utilising the power of your unconscious mind as you re-wire it to resist and resurface your receptive self with that non-stick finish.

You are changing your surface from Velcro to Teflon.

Through the techniques and exercises in this book, you will begin to separate the problematic behaviour that has attached itself to you through stress response from that part of you which is responsible for that behaviour.

In other words, new choices of behaviour are being established by having that part of you take responsibility for implementing other behaviours that will satisfy the same positive intention but without the problem by-products of the old behaviour.

By breaking up the established, learned template you can create a situation whereby that part of you will have a choice of the old behaviour or a new behaviour.

It's still a choice, rather than a compulsion, but that old behaviour became a compulsion and humanity is all about choice, isn't it?

For example, where part of you used to worry about a future event, such as an interview or an exam or a meeting, now that part of you can decide to use visualisation to rehearse a positive outcome so that your brain will start to believe a different outcome is possible.

Likewise, where part of you used to eat food or smoke cigarettes in order to release the brain chemicals such as endorphins so that you felt good, that part of you can decide to take exercise or deep breathing or go to a comedy show and have a good laugh instead.

Every person is made up of many parts. Like a car, all the parts have to function together in harmony for the whole vehicle to start up and move along the road.

If one part is malfunctioning, the whole car will struggle to perform.

It may be that a spark plug has become clogged up with carbon deposits to the point that it sparks dysfunctionally and thus it throws out the timing of the firing sequence resulting in the car running roughly.

It may be that a tyre has attracted a stone or a nail that causes a slow puncture and the car gradually becomes less easy to keep on a straight line.

There are many instances where one part breaks down and the whole just simply won't go at all.

We wonder how it can be that the while vehicle can fail when all that's broken down is one little spark plug!

Like the car, humans are a sum of parts.

The main parts are generally recognised as the physical body, the core self and the various aspects of the personality.

Self-awareness (the Watching Self) has the ability to "see" both the body and the personality and is unique to humans.

Depending on your culture and beliefs, our "trinity" may be referred to as body, soul and spirit or similar.

We know about the Watching Self because most of us are able to adjust our personality to suit different situations.

So through the Watching Self, we can identify that "part" which has the stress attached to it.

We can then work to assist that part in detaching the stress, like Velcro, through offering a choice of different behaviours that may produce the same result in terms of good feelings.

Break Out!

Every one of us has addictive behaviours. It's good to identify them.

Allow your unconscious mind to come up with a behaviour that you might consider, if you were being really honest with yourself, could be addictive or could become addictive.

It may be related to food, or drink, or drugs, or the Internet, or something completely different.

Now consider which part of you that behaviour is attached to.

What was the anchor or stimulus or moment in life when that kicked in?

For example, when I was a teenager I was generally very easy going and prided myself in not getting easily embarrassed and this enabled me to be a great salesperson.

One day, and I still remember it vividly; I was walking across a road on my way to my office when I was suddenly aware of a new feeling being somehow "beamed" into my brain.

I suddenly, at that one moment, seemed to have a feeling of fear programmed into me, directly from somewhere outside of myself.

From that moment on, at the age of 18, I had to deal with anxiety and worry, later diagnosed as a fear of the future that for many years required medication.

How did that happen?

Why did that happen?

Actually, I now know that I don't need to know why, because that moment can be dealt with through a change of perspective so it doesn't have the bearing on my life that it once had.

However, for you, there will be a moment in time when your stress-induced problem behaviour took root.

Take a deep breath and allow that moment to come to mind.

It may take a while, but your unconscious mind is aware of it so it will bring it to your attention.

Remember not to dwell on the past. When the moment comes, just hold that thought.

When you've got it, try to identify which part of you it is attached to.

Is it your body (physical) or your personality (cognitive)?

Either way, you can utilise moving into your Watching Self perspective to unhook it.

Close your eyes now and go inside and relax.

Take three deep breaths and allow all other thoughts to drift away, up and away like they are attached to coloured toy balloons with little tags on each is written that thought.

Now focus on that problem behaviour.

What feelings does it produce now?

Make those feelings stronger.

Focus in and identify where they are attached and if they produce a physical or a mental response.

Think what you could offer as a choice of a different behaviour that might produce the same feelings.

Perhaps base it on one of the earlier exercises.

Maybe the alternative behaviour is something you used to do which made you feel good which you have just stopped doing.

Try this technique to help to unhook that behaviour from the part you've recognised.

Now think about that problem behaviour again.

How does it feel now?

By just becoming aware of the issue, you have begun to loosen the grip of that behaviour which had attached itself to a part of you. You have also identified the part it was attached to.

You may not realise it now, but you have created a situation whereby you have given that part of you a choice in the future.

When the moment arises when you would normally, almost automatically find yourself doing what you did, you may find that you are thinking about it now.

What you can do next is introduce a new choice that will produce the old feeling but in a more acceptable, healthier way.

Ok, come back now and take a deep breath and relax.

Think of something completely different to reboot your mind.

Once you free up that part to have choices, you are on the road to success and as you change your motivations so you will see true results.

This is because motivation, or lack of it, can be a cultural thing.

For example, I was enjoying a Chinese meal with some friends and at the end of the meal the owner of the restaurant came over to our table and offered us some green tea.

Normally, at home, I would take green tea from a tea bag, very much as you would any other form of tea.

But this experience was amazing.

The restaurant owner brought out a collection of tiny china cups and containers of various shapes together with a large teapot and two smaller teapots.

He then proceeded to explain to us the history of his actions as he poured water from one pot to another and then over the fresh tea plant and then into one small container that we then had to pour into another small cup before drinking.

The restaurant owner was fascinating to watch and he undertook his task with pure pleasure and a precision and commitment normally reserved for defusing a bomb!

What spoke to me was his commitment and respect for his culture.

Seldom do we take time in our modern culture to enjoy such activities.

In the UK generally, tea is taken in a plastic or polystyrene container, on the run, between meetings. We seldom taste it, and when we do it's normally pretty disgusting.

But if we were to take more pride and time over the simplest activity, perhaps we would regain some of the interest in the smaller things in life, which really can be quite good fun.

That restaurant owner got immense satisfaction from serving us as his guests.

Many people when suffering from stress tend to turn their focus inwards and can actually stop doing things they used to once enjoy such as exercising, dancing, doing sports, going out and being with friends.

The stress response can take so much energy just to maintain that there's sometimes precious little spare capacity to go out and enjoy life.

It all seems too much effort, especially if negative thinking has kicked in.

That "what's the point" attitude can really undermine your life and ability to engage and have fun with situation you once took on with relish.

In the latter part of the last century there was a great psychotherapist and hypnotherapist, Milton H Erickson. Erickson was a master at observing human behaviour and identifying unique resources in his patients that he then used to help them change their perspectives on life.

There is a story about a lady whom Erickson was treating who was suffering from depression.

When chatting with her prior to treatment, she told him that she loved flowers and used to grow African violets.

She also said that she had once been active in the church. Both activities, along with most other external facing activities had ceased as her depression had got hold of her.

Erickson believed that a person's problem could be separated from the core person so they could begin to unhook that behaviour and find the freedom they once enjoyed.

He encouraged the lady to grow violets again and also to start to give them as gifts to people from the church that had become unwell.

Her "ministry" became a great source of healing not just for those she gave the flowers but also herself.

The "African Violet Lady" was cured of her depression by returning to that which she had once loved.

This story illustrates a great reframe by the therapist and someone effectively borrowing another's ability to see things from a different perspective to "jump start" their mind to get back to creative thinking and enjoying life.

Break Out!

Think of an activity you used to really enjoy which you have stopped doing.

Why did you stop?

Close your eyes and go inside.

Take a deep breath and relax.

In your mind, count down from 10 to 1 and as you do, imagine travelling down in an elevator.

On the count of 1, the doors open and you walk out into a huge department store.

People seem to be coming and going, buying goods.

They all seem to be happy and smiling, chatting amongst themselves.

Your attention is brought to a sign above a particular counter.

The sign reads, "Rediscovery".

You approach the counter and notice a doorway just to the side that has a sign on the door.

On the sign is your name.

You enter through the door and walk into a large park under a clear blue sky.

You become aware of the warm breeze and a scent of flowers.

You notice a group of people by a fountain of clear water seemingly enjoying themselves in the afternoon sunshine.

One of the people looks a lot like you.

Notice how much fun they are having as they laugh and play with the others.

Watch for a while and then walk to the fountain and take a long drink.

Now you attention is drawn to a set of steps leading towards a domed building on the top of a shallow hill.

As you follow the path up the hill you can see that group of people and that person who looks like you down below.

They are sitting in a group now on the grass, still laughing and having fun.

You stand before the domed building.

Above the door of the building is a sign that reads, "Freedom".

The wooden door opens freely as you push it and you enter.

You find yourself back in the department store by the lift door.

Re-entering the lift, you press the button for the 10th floor.

As you travel up in the lift, count up from 1 to 10 and as you do, you will notice a lightness as the energy that is in that water from the fountain of life to you.

Breathe deeply and relax.

Open your eyes.

And focus outwards.

You are on your journey from stress to success.

Timelines and Your Future Resources

Focus on the outcome but enjoy the journey.

Why wait for some external event to make you happy?

So many people just don't enjoy the journey of their lives, concentrating so much on the destination; they can miss a whole stream of events that occur along the way.

You'll know when you've reached your destination!

Have you ever admired someone as they've gone about their job, such as a craftsman working on a piece of furniture, a sportsperson, an artist or a TV presenter? Perhaps you have admired an actor, a politician or a comedian?

Your brain has a unique way of working, as it matches innate or learnt templates to patterns it recognises in the external environment. For example, a baby, soon after it's born, is seeking to complete the feeding need by matching its instinctive template with the mother's nipple or the teat of the bottle containing milk.

If you put your finger near the baby's mouth, it may "latch on" and suck on it. This indicates that the template / stimulus pattern matching is not specific, but general. The baby will continue to suck, but after a time, when no milk is forthcoming from the finger, will cry as it is still hungry.

As we grow and learn, we pick up new templates for which we seek external stimulus to match to.

These could be something like walking, quite a dramatic step, literally. But it could also be opening a door, which again indicates a general pattern match. Once we have learned how to open one door, we can usually open most doors, assuming they open by way of a handle. A sliding door will require a new skill to be learned, but we don't then assume all doors from that point on will be sliding.

We now have two type of door and we have to assess, when confronted with a door, which of the two learned patterns will be appropriate.

If we are unsure, we will probably project the third positive image to cover any embarrassment we may experience by choosing the wrong option to open the door.

Humans learn by watching others.

If you admire another, you will seek to learn from them.

That is how we come to have heroes, or idols.

Early in life our parents or family can be such people we look up to and learn from. Later in life they tend to be people we work with or, as previously mentioned, people from TV or films.

Now, as your brain does not really know the difference between a real and a vividly imagined event, you can set up a model or mentor at any time, be it a real person, TV or film personality or, amazingly, even yourself.

Now you have practiced and perfected the skill and technique of visualisation, you can set up any form of model in your imagination and watch them in action.

Your brain will automatically set up a desire to be like that person.

Your brain also seeks completion. If you set it a task, it will seek to complete it.

This is where dreaming comes in. If you go to bed with unresolved issues or non-discharged emotions arising from events of the day, you may well dream about it.

In management terms, your brain is the perfect "completer/finisher".

Your brain will set up a scenario, a sort of play pieced together from stored memories, because you dream with your eyes closed, in which you will act out unresolved issues.

Due to the general nature of pattern matching, the brain's scenarios will be metaphorical representations of events you have experienced during the day.

The brain's innate requirement to seek completion is what makes us such great problem solvers and completers of tasks.

When you set up a model in your imagination, and create a desire to be like that model, your brain will programme itself to undertake and complete that task.

The amazing thing is that you yourself can be that model.

You can programme your own brain to make you the person you imagine yourself to be!

Sometimes it is actually more effective to model yourself against a group rather than a person.

For example, if you want to be a great scholar, an academic genius, then it's better to model yourself to a group of graduates receiving their certificates than Albert Einstein.

The group is something your brain can set up a template to work towards.

There is no specific person but a classification to aim for.

You are setting up a future timeline for which the result is academic qualification, not the individual known as Albert Einstein.

There are lots of graduates.

There's only one Einstein.

However, when it comes to visualising most improvements then you can use yourself in a future situation as a model to set a new template.

Break Out!

Sit in a comfortable position with both feet on the floor.

Close your eyes and go "inside".

Take a deep breath in and as you breathe out, let go and relax.

Think of standing at your bathroom mirror cleaning your teeth tomorrow morning.

Where is the image in your mind's eye?

Is it inside your head, outside, to the right, left, in front or behind?

Now do the same for one week in the future.

Now one month in the future.

Now six months.

Now one year.

You now have a timeline – a series of images stretching around or out from your present position.

Ok, now think of where you want your life to be in one year's time.

What will you have achieved?

Where will you be living?

Will you be in a new job?

Have new relationships?

Be real with yourself.

Now install an image of your ideal self in a year's time in that farthest position in your timeline.

Really make it your ideal self.

Happy, confident, healthy and successful.

Now think of the three major milestones you had to achieve to reach your ideal situation in one year's time.

Place those milestones in place of the images you had in your timeline at one week, one month and six months into the future.

You should now have four images moving along your timeline to your ideal goal in one year's time.

Now make each of those images bigger, given them more colour, make them widescreen movies.

Now begin to drift into your first image.

As you become completely associated, see what you see and hear what you hear and notice the feelings associated with your first stage of success on your timeline.

Do the same for one month, six months, until you reach your ideal goal a year ahead.

Just pause and watch yourself for a moment.

See how good you look and how much at ease and in control you are.

Now step into that ideal you as you receive the accolades and rewards for this year's achievements.

How good does that feel?

Remember when you used to get stressed just thinking about tomorrow?

How far have you come?

And now you can drift back to the present.

OK, come back out, take a deep breath, let go and open your eyes.

Before you come back completely, allow your experience to become a reality in your mind.

Just sit for a few minutes and imagine that timeline is being downloaded and installed into your brain from the universe around you just like a computer programme from the Internet.

You created that whole thing with your mind, just in exactly the same way as a software engineer designs that programme for you to download from the net.

The Internet has enabled us to think differently.

But it was just the object of someone's creating mind.

You have created your ideal timeline.

So make sure it's installed now and your brain will begin to work towards completing the programme.

When you're happy that programme is settled in your mind, think of something completely different to reboot your mind.

There's another exercise that you can do with a friend or partner that is great fun.

This is also a timeline exercise but it gives an alternative option to a similar outcome.

This is best done with a partner who will "interview" you on your successful achievement one year from now.

Imagine your ideal goal, what you want to achieve in one year's time.

Imagine you are there, one year ahead, having achieved your goal.

Now write down the major steps you had to achieve to get to your goal.

For example, if it were building your own house, you would have to get some land, obtain permission to build, arrange the money, arrange the contractors etc.

When you are happy with your steps, ask your partner to interview you about your success from the point a year in the future.

As you answer, be utterly convincing about your achievements.

Your partner should write down all the steps.

Once they have all the steps, you close your eyes and they feed back to you all those steps and as they do use your Reality Simulator to create a fully immersive experience as if you were inside each scenario.

Notice the details and how you feel at each stage.

Get your partner to interview you again while you still keep your eyes closed.

They should ask you deeply detailed questions such as

"What was it that people around you noticed when you achieved that stage?"

Or "how does it make you feel that you have achieved all this?"

You will find this is a rich experience that will also begin to lay down templates for future direction.

And the even better news is that the *Law of Attraction* at work in the universe is also now on notice that you have laid down a new set of rules!

More for the journey in the next module.

Maintaining Success

Attitude

Wouldn't it be great if thinking of work elicited the same emotions and feelings as your favourite leisure activity or vacation?

Why shouldn't it?

Remember, you have the control!

Is it a fear of being different?

Well that's really no excuse any more, is it?

Because now you are different!

This is just one of those old behaviour patterns and now you have a choice. You can choose how you will feel about any given situation.

Remember, there is always at least one way through any difficulty.

Think of at least two solutions, at least two ways through a situation.

Don't think of them as Plan A and Plan B, think of them both as Plan A, they're both as relevant and they both provide you with a great outcome.

So why not have three Plan A's?

Every which way, you win!

WHY NOT?

Come on, have some fun.

You don't need to see things the same way anymore and really, by seeing life from different perspectives and angles you can still make a huge difference in your life and others too.

WHY NOT?

Make it your mantra!

WHY NOT?

If you don't buy a ticket, you won't win the lottery.

If you don't get the key out of your pocket you'll never open the door.

There are endless doors waiting to be opened.

I just want to run through a few techniques to help you maintain the success you will have achieved to date and to cement the success path you have created in your unconscious mind.

You will also be pleased to know that throughout the world there will be others who have also begun a new path to success through the new direction you have chosen.

Set out right now to prepare your own Stress to Success survival pack

You choose what's best for your own pack, but here are some reminders and suggestions:

Firstly, breathing is vital to maintaining relaxation and relaxation is vital to maintaining control. You will be able to make clearer choices, your memory will function more efficiently and you will find more time and space in your reaction and response mechanism to think more creatively.

Keep 7/11 breathing in the readily accessible part of your Stress to Success survival pack.

Remember, breathe in to the count of 7, and breathe out to the count of 11.

It's the same activity a smoker employs to create that relaxed feeling; drag in through the mouth, exhale through the nose. Only you are doing it without the toxic chemicals entering your system, hijacking your brain and clouding your mind.

Secondly, remember to keep control of your Perspective and use that to understand how others feel in given situations.

Always be prepared to "float about" into people around you to gain new perspectives and understand how others think, operate and see things.

Thirdly, watch your <u>Diet</u> but don't do dieting!

Fourthly, <u>Laugh</u> as much as you can – release those endorphins!

Fifthly, be aware of exposure to negative <u>Media</u>!

There's a children's Bible song that includes these very wise words:

Be careful little eyes, what you see

Be careful little ears what you hear

Be careful little mouth what you say

Be careful little hands what you touch

Be careful little feet where you go

Wise words indeed!

The sixth maintenance technique is to always <u>finish</u> what you start because this will give you a real sense of achievement, whatever the outcome, and helps maintain a healthy self-image.

Remember to watch out for motivation when it comes to setting <u>Targets</u>.

Is the target you have to achieve your own or someone else's?

If it's your own, then don't demand too much of yourself.

If it's someone else's make sure you have agreed to outcomes that are achievable.

If you have a boss or a partner who is manipulating you to do what you just don't want to do or feeding you negative messages then create a <u>Negativity Shield</u>.

Break Out!

Close your eyes and go inside.

Do a 7/11 breathing exercise for a couple of minutes.

Now think about all the positive energy you have created through doing the exercises in this book.

Let those positive feelings swell up inside you.

Double the intensity and give them a bright colour as they spread throughout your body.

Do some more 7/11 breathing.

Think of a time when you were completely in control of your life.

Remember a time when you were completely happy and everything was going your way.

Really enter into that time.

Notice the feelings, which way they move through your body and spin them faster.

Make the feeling stronger still.

Press your thumb and finger together to create an anchor and as you do this make the feeling twice as strong again.

Now let the feeling spread through your skin creating an impenetrable barrier around you, like a suit of armour.

You can smile now, because you have the control.

You have the switch.

When you bring that thumb and finger together you will remember those feelings and switch on that negativity shield which even the most depressive, miserable, manipulative person will not be able to penetrate with their suggestions!

Remember, you have the control.

OK, open your eyes, come back and think of something else to reboot your mind.

Finally, I have a theory which may need you to be even more creative than ever in your thinking but if you go with it, could absolutely blow away the last fragments of belief that you cannot be in control of your own destiny.

I heard recently about experiments in Quantum Physics that got me thinking about the way we create our reality and I would like to share this here because it will not only help to illustrate my next point, it may also help you to grasp the implications of what I'm saying even if taken metaphorically.

In very simple terms, and for the purpose of this book, there is a theory that some objects are, in a way linked, and no matter if they are separated and how far apart the distance of that separation may be.

For example, yoghurt is a culture that feeds on milk. If the culture is separated and one part is fed milk, the other will match the digestive process even though it is not receiving milk, but somehow it is "aware" that its counterpart is.

Huge distances may separate these cultures with no apparent effect on the digestive process.

It is said that when objects separated by distance respond simultaneously they are "spinning".

Now, remember in an earlier chapter I suggested that everything created starts with a thought in the human mind?

Well, what if those thoughts are not unique,
but inspired by another, by a partner thought
somewhere else on the earth?

What if when you get an inspired thought, your
mind is just simply spinning in harmony with
another?

And what if you are meant to seek out that other
to complete the creation of a whole idea?

What if there are more than two?

What if there are dozens, perhaps hundreds,
or perhaps thousands who all have a similar
inspiration and then begin to seek each other out
to complete the process of creation or cultural
evolution?

Now consider the immense power of the Internet
in bringing people together at the speed of light?

What if, on receipt of an inspired idea, you
"Googled" to find that others had received the
same inspired idea?

There is power in agreement.

There is a power in attraction.

We seem to be on the verge of a breakthrough in
understanding how the world community can
communicate and the universe appears to operate

on quantum principles and there is a tremendously powerful law of attraction at work.

After all, once you've planted the seed, you watch the plant grow don't you? A tree will generally grow towards the sun.

Start thinking differently when you plant your seeds!

I'm going to leave it there because this is basically a practical book on beating stress and making a success of your life, not a physics handbook.

However, I would suggest that as you dwell on those creative thoughts you have had recently, it might be worth harnessing the power of the internet to see if there's anyone else out there that you should be in contact with.

To quote another Biblical passage out of context, "There is nothing new under the sun".

I this book I have busted three myths about stress.

Quite simply there are three common misconceptions about three things that can quite easily become replacements for natural stress-busting methods suggested in this book, such as proper breathing, eating and understanding life from different perspectives.

I have quoted a couple of Biblical principles and I have one other one to offer you.

"Treat others as you would want to be treated yourself"

Perhaps that's just another way of looking at perspectives.

Three activities people adopt assuming that they help their stress are smoking, drinking and drugs.

In the long term;
1. Smoking tobacco does not reduce stress!
2. Drinking alcohol does not reduce stress!
3. Taking drugs does not reduce stress!

Smoking is a substitute for proper breathing and the release of endorphins, the brain's "happy" chemicals. It hijacks endorphin production so you become dependent on the cigarettes for stress management that you are quite capable of doing with your natural resources.

Drinking alcohol screws up your sleeping patterns and interferes with your blood sugar levels. You then become dependent on the alcohol to provide the "fix" needed to manage stress that you could have done much more easily from your own resources had you not drunk it in the first place.

And finally, what are drugs if they are not some form of manufactured way of managing your stressful life. Why do you want to be dependent upon something made by another human being when you have your own resources to do that for no cost at all?

Just change your perspective.

You have all the resources you need.

Funny that, isn't it? You have been provided with a vehicle to move around this planet and all the fuel it needs to keep going and all the tools it needs to keep functioning.

Now you have a road map as well.

So enjoy the journey.

You'll know when you've reached your destination.

From stress to success!

Lightning Source UK Ltd.
Milton Keynes UK
UKOW051853161211

183942UK00002B/9/P